# WRITING WITH A WORD PROCESSOR

*Books by William Zinsser*

Any Old Place with You
Seen Any Good Movies Lately?
The City Dwellers
Weekend Guests
The Haircurl Papers
Pop Goes America
The Paradise Bit
The Lunacy Boom
On Writing Well
Writing with a Word Processor

# Writing
# with a
# Word
# Processor

## William Zinsser

HARPER & ROW, PUBLISHERS, New York
Cambridge, Philadelphia, San Francisco, London
Mexico City, São Paulo, Sydney
1817

The incidents in this book that involve IBM employees are true, but the names have been changed. The author has no connection of any kind with IBM except as an individual customer.

W. Z.

WRITING WITH A WORD PROCESSOR. Copyright © 1983 by William K. Zinsser. All rights reserved. Printed in the United States of America. No part of this book may be used or reproduced in any manner whatsoever without written permission except in the case of brief quotations embodied in critical articles and reviews. For information address Harper & Row, Publishers, Inc., 10 East 53rd Street, New York, N.Y. 10022. Published simultaneously in Canada by Fitzhenry & Whiteside Limited, Toronto.

*Designer: Sidney Feinberg*

---

Library of Congress Cataloging in Publication Data

Zinsser, William Knowlton.
    Writing with a word processor.

    1. Authorship—Data processing.    2. Word processing
(Office practice)    I. Title.
PN171.D37Z56    1983            808'.02'02854            82-48140
ISBN 0-06-015055-6                83 84 85 86 87 10 9 8 7 6 5 4 3
ISBN 0-06-091060-7                83 84 85 86 87 10 9 8 7 6 5 4

---

# Contents

# Preface

Maybe I'm not the last person in the world who would be expected to write with a word processor, but I'm one of the last. I belong to a generation of writers and editors who think of paper and pencil as holy objects. I taught myself to type at the age of ten and ever since have been banging out words onto paper, and then crossing them out and penciling other words in, and then retyping what I had revised. The feel of paper is important to me. I have always thought that a writer should have physical contact with the materials of his craft—that he should be able to spread out his notes and his early drafts and to work on them with his sacred pencil.

So how does it happen that I find myself tapping out these words on a computer keyboard and watching them appear on a terminal screen? The screen is black and the words are green—hardly my usual colors—and I have no paper anywhere. I have separated myself from paper. I'm wholly in the hands of a machine. I don't even like machines. I am not mechanical. I don't understand how mechanical objects work, and I can't fix things with my hands. I never was the typical American boy who had to have the latest gadget. Gadgets fluster me. I can't open a childproof medicine bottle. I never know which button to push—or is it pull?—at the laundromat. I can't even tell where to insert the coin in a Coke machine; kind strangers help me out as I try to wedge a quarter into some chrome device that appears to be a coin slot but isn't. They look at me with a mixture of pity and amazement.

Nor do I understand written instructions. Am I the only American car driver, for instance, who can't figure out how to heat or cool the car? The lever that operates this mechanism is in a slot that offers these choices: COOL, NORM-MAX, AVG, HI-LO, VENT and HEAT. How can one selection give me both HI and LO? How does HI differ from HEAT, or from MAX? What is VENT doing in this spectrum of temperatures? Who is NORM? I have almost never found the right amount of heat for my car except by chance. The temperature somehow rises to MAX and I open all the windows to compensate. Surely this is not what Detroit had in mind.

For such a mechanical boob to decide to write on a word processor would seem to be a sure invitation to despair. The word processor is, after all, a computer, and most people are scared of computers. Most people are also scared of the act of writing; even the professional writer faces his daily task with a nervousness that never quite goes away. I didn't know what would happen when the fear of computers got combined with the fear of writing. But I did know that the word processor was here to stay. And I knew that if I could master it, anybody could.

# 1.  Personal Baggage

I first realized that the act of writing was about to enter a new era five years ago when I went to see an editor at *The New York Times*. As I was ushered through the vast city room I felt that I had strayed into the wrong office. The place was clean and carpeted and quiet. As I passed long rows of desks I saw that almost every desk had its own computer terminal and its own solemn occupant—a man or a woman typing at the computer keyboard or reading what was on the terminal screen. I saw no typewriters, no paper, no mess. It was a cool and sterile environment; the drones at their machines could have been processing insurance claims or tracking a spacecraft in orbit. What they didn't look like were newspaper people, and what the place didn't look like was a newspaper office.

I knew how a newspaper office should look and sound and smell—I worked in one for thirteen years. The paper was the *New York Herald Tribune*, and its city room, wide as a city block, was dirty and disheveled. Reporters wrote on ancient typewriters that filled the air with clatter; copy editors labored on coffee-stained desks over what the reporters had written. Crumpled balls of paper littered the floor and filled the wastebaskets—failed efforts to write a good lead or a decent sentence. The walls were grimy—every few years they were painted over in a less restful shade of eye-rest green—and the atmosphere was hazy with the smoke of cigarettes and cigars. At the very center the city editor, a giant named L. L. Engelking, bellowed his displeasure with the day's work, his voice a rumbling volcano in our lives. I thought it was the most beautiful place in the world.

I had always wanted to be a newspaperman, and the *Herald Tribune* was the newspaper I wanted to be a man on. As a boy I had been reared on the *"Trib,"* and its Bodoni Bold headlines and beautiful makeup fixed themselves early in my mind as exactly how a newspaper should present itself to the world. The same mixture of craftsmanship and warmth ran through the writing. A *Herald Tribune* story always had some extra dimension of humor or humanity, or surprise, or graceful execution, that didn't turn up in other papers. The people who put this paper together obviously worked with care and loved the work. My dream was to be one of them.

As a teen-ager I wrote for the school newspaper and learned to set type at the local shop where the paper was printed. The afternoons I spent there were some of the happiest of my boyhood. I loved the smell of the ink and the clacking of the linotype machines. I liked being part of a physical process that took what I wrote and converted it into type and locked it in a frame and put it on a press and printed it for anybody to read. One Christmas I asked my parents for a printing press—a wish that they must have regretted granting, for it was installed in the attic, directly over their room, and the house shook at night with irregular thumps as I fed paper into the press and pulled its huge handle down. I bought books on type and studied the different typefaces, learning how type cutters and printers over the centuries had shaped the letters to achieve legibility and a certain emotional weight.

At college I was editor of a campus magazine, and I hung around the university press where it was composed and printed. I was hooked on a tradition. Even when I left college during World War II to enlist in the army I didn't escape the process of getting the day's events validated on paper. Colonel McCloskey, finding a captive writer (and a mere sergeant) in his midst, took no chance that his feats of command might go unrecorded. He commanded me to write the company history, and, sitting in a wintry tent in Italy with an old typewriter and a lot of paper, I did.

After the war when I went looking for a job I inevitably went looking at the *Herald Tribune*, and when I heard George Cornish, the managing editor, offering to hire me as a beginning reporter at forty-five dollars a week I considered myself as rich as Rockefeller. Well, almost. The paper in those first postwar years was a constellation of journalists at the top of their form. I still remember the routine excellence of the local reporters and foreign correspondents and the elegance of the critics and columnists: Virgil Thomson, Red Smith, Walter Lippmann and many others. It was a paper whose editors coveted good writing. Not only did they publish the best writers; they cultivated good writing in younger members of the staff by showing that they cared. Those older men who made us rewrite what we had written—and rewritten—weren't doing it only for our own good but for the honorableness of the craft. They were custodians of a trust.

Surrounded by veteran reporters, I studied their habits and was struck by their fierce pride. The *Herald Tribune* always had less money and a smaller staff than its august competitor, *The New York Times*. Nevertheless it was an article of faith that one *Trib* reporter could cover a story as well as the three *Times* reporters assigned to the same beat. Nobody exemplified this idea more than Peter Kihss, who was covering the newly established United Nations in New York. He wasn't just a member of the *Trib's* United Nations bureau; he *was* the bureau, and every afternoon he came back staggering under heavy reports issued by the UN's burgeoning agencies and committees. He then sat down at his ancient typewriter, which he pounded with demonic speed, and wrote two or three articles that put into coherent form everything important that the UN had done that day. He was a man possessed by facts.

Though I didn't know it at the time, those years were the end of an era for the *Herald Tribune*. High costs and various other factors began to erode the paper's quality, and over the next decade the stars gradually left and went elsewhere, correctly sensing that the *Trib's* sickness of body and soul would be terminal. Some reporters went over to *The New York Times*, including Peter Kihss, whose by-line continued to be a warranty of truth doggedly pursued.

When my own turn came to leave the *Herald Tribune*—I resigned to become a free-lance writer—I also took plenty of baggage along from my apprenticeship with editors and printers whose standards were high. I found that I was never quite satisfied with what I had written; I had a compulsion to rewrite, to polish, to cut, to start over. This meant that I not only did a lot of rewriting; I also did a lot of retyping. At the end of the day my wastebasket was full and my back and shoulders were stiff.

My family quite properly urged me to get an electric typewriter, and I tried one out. It drove me crazy. My touch was far too heavy from all the years of pummeling an Underwood; the electric typewriter, designed for gentler hands, kept putting spaces within the words as well as between the words. M y se nt e nces lo oke d some ething lik e th is, and I spent more time erasing—and swearing—than writing. I also didn't like the typewriter's steady hum; I hate unwanted noise, and I didn't want it as part of the writing process. The job is hard enough in silence.

But during the 1970s I began to realize that everything I knew about printing—the process of getting words on paper—was becoming obsolete. Gutenberg was through. His invention of movable type had changed the world and lasted five hundred years. Now nobody wanted Gutenberg's "hot type." The new thing was "cold type"—type that didn't exist as type at all, but only as an image on film. Magazine writers continued to write on a typewriter, but the person who "set" their articles no longer sat at a linotype machine. He sat at a keyboard that put the words on tape, and the tape somehow got converted into film. The proofs that came back from the printer no longer had the bite of type into paper; they looked like what they were—photographs of type. Something had been lost: the clean edge of letters, the age-old flavor of craft.

But a great deal had also been gained. With actual type eliminated, a whole series of cumbersome and expensive steps was bypassed: setting the type, arranging it in flat pages, and making curved plates from those pages that could be fastened onto high-speed rotary presses. Just compose the type on film—call it "photocomposition"—and fasten the film to the presses. Eureka!

Still, I assumed that writers couldn't be plugged into this system. Writers were human—they couldn't be wired like machines. (This is not to say that some writers aren't very peculiarly wired.) And yet—portents were in the air. A few friends who worked for newspapers told me that their papers were "converting to terminals." What could that mean? It seemed to mean that writers could be plugged into the system after all. If typesetting could be done on film (saving the time and cost of setting real type), writing could be done on film (saving the time and cost of having someone retype on film what the reporter had written on paper). Just take the reporter's paper away and sit him down in front of a new kind of computer. Call it a word processor. Process that reporter's words right out of his brain and into an electronic circuit. Eureka again.

This was the new stage that journalism had reached when I went to see the *New York Times* editor in 1978. The paper had just completed a radical conversion of its plant: the editorial rooms had been torn apart to accommodate sophisticated new wiring and equipment. I had heard talk of the chaos that accompanied the change, but I hadn't really pictured what the new city room would look like. Maybe I didn't want to know. Now I knew. As I walked between the long rows of reporters at their silent terminals my journalistic past evaporated.

I asked the *Times* editor how the reporters were adjusting to the new procedure. He said that of course they all hated it at first, especially the older ones. They kicked and screamed and said they could never write on these terminals. But after a few weeks they began to feel comfortable, and now most of them said they never wanted to go back to a typewriter. He said the reporters really liked being able to instantly revise what they wrote, deleting or inserting or moving words and phrases and whole sentences and seeing their work always neat and tidy on the screen. He pointed out that not only were the writers doing their writing on the screen; that was also where the editors were editing all the copy. They summoned the reporters' articles on *their* screens, making their own changes, as editors will.

I wondered how this would affect the subtle relationship between writers and editors. I thought of all the times when a *Herald Tribune* editor brought over a piece of my copy to discuss changes he had made or wanted to make, and of all the times when I—as an editor or a teacher—had gone over my changes with a young writer or a student. To be apprenticed to a good editor is the best way to learn how to write. What would happen when all the editing was done on film by successive editors? Who would know who had done what? Who would remember what the original copy said? And who would be accountable for what had been changed? Nobody's handwriting—or fingerprints—would survive to tell the tale.

These were questions that I would want to know more about. But for the present I had seen enough of the future, and I started to leave. As I was walking back out of the city room my eye was caught by an unusual sight. In the middle of a row of desks with reporters working at terminals I saw one reporter writing on an old standard typewriter. He was a gray-haired man, obviously near retirement. Just as obviously he had rebelled against learning the new technology and had been granted special dispensation to stick with the venerable tools of his trade. I looked at him with sympathy and with a certain admiration: the last puritan, true to his values. The more I looked, the more familiar he seemed. There was something about the intensity with which he peered through his thick metal-framed glasses at what he was writing, something about the ferocious energy with which he attacked the typewriter keys. I had seen this reporter before.

Then I realized where I had seen him. It was Peter Kihss.

# 2. Entering the Future

The sight of Pete Kihss lingered with me. I identified with him more than I cared to admit. Just because America's newspapers were forcing their reporters and editors into electronic bondage for production reasons of their own, I as an individual writer didn't have to join the stampede. What set writers apart as individuals was their individuality. I had been getting along fine with my old Underwood, and I wasn't about to change.

But the notion of writers at their word processors started to tug at my consciousness. When I watched *Lou Grant* on television I no longer thought it was odd to see reporters writing at a terminal. And I began to see word processors in magazine layouts and Sunday newspaper sections devoted to home decoration. Designers were tastefully accommodating them in the study, where, only yesterday, nothing vulgar had been allowed to intrude on the quiet elegance of the antique desk, the leather-bound dictionary and the glass paperweight holding down the day's genteel mail.

I also began to hear about real authors writing real books on their own word processors. Jimmy Carter went home to Plains to write his memoirs on a word processor: the first

President to go electronic. (If Lincoln had had one for the Gettysburg Address he probably would have deleted "Four score and seven years ago" and made it "87." Thank God he wrote the sonorous phrase by hand and didn't want to erase it.) Suddenly all the magazines were running cover stories about "the computer in your life." In only a few years, we were told, everybody in America would be sitting at the keyboard paying bills, instructing his bank and his broker, heating his home and pool, calculating his calories, playing the horses and presumably programming a satisfying sex life.

Meanwhile the word processor had invaded the American office, welcomed as a miraculous savior by every executive whose business required the same clusters of words to be neatly typed again and again. Law firms, for instance, with their long and lugubrious paragraphs of "boilerplate," could simply store these standardized blocks in the memory of the machine and call them up and insert them wherever they were needed. Architects started using the word processor for specifications, and doctors for medical reports.

It was also a Godsend for all the businesses that depend on correspondence with their customers—mail-order houses, for example, that receive a daily flood of special orders, queries and complaints. Now they could store all the paragraphs that answer all the routine queries (the item is out of stock, there will be a delay of several weeks, the product has been discontinued, we regret the inconvenience), plus the gracious opening and closing paragraphs that thank the customer for writing and for being such a faithful friend.

Clearly the day was not far off when vast numbers of Americans would be writing on word processors—not just "writers," but all the people who had to do any writing to transact the ordinary business of the day. This would be especially true as the nation's secretarial pool continued to dry up. Five years ago it was common for two middle managers to share a secretary; today the ratio is as high as fifteen to one. Good managers can no longer afford to wait for an available secretary to type a memo; they will write their memos on a word processor and transmit them instantly to the company's out-of-town offices, where other managers will read them on a terminal and answer them. Writing on a word processor, in short, would soon become second nature.

All this I began to know objectively. But subjectively it still didn't touch me. Word processors were what happened to somebody else.

Then, one day, my wife said, "You ought to write a book about how to write with a word processor."

"Who?" I said. "*Me?*"

# 3.   A Shopping Trip

The next day I bit the bullet and went around to IBM. Actually it was two weeks later. I'm not good at biting bullets—I tend to put off tasks like going to the dentist and to IBM.

I chose IBM solely on the basis of its reputation as an old and respected leader in its field. I knew that many companies were now making word processors. But I didn't want to waste time comparing their products because I had no basis of comparison. I proceeded on the assumption that all word processors were fundamentally alike. Some of their functions would differ in minor ways, and so would their keyboards and much of their terminology. I could only describe how my machine worked and leave it to readers to adapt my experience to their own. I would rent or buy my equipment from IBM as an individual customer, not as a writer making a business arrangement. There would be no discounts or special favors; nobody would owe anybody anything. My book would imply no endorsement of IBM over any other company's equipment.

All these practical and ethical details were clear to me as I went to an IBM showroom to meet the product face to face. But nothing else was clear. My head was clogged with anxiety and resistance. I really did feel as if I were going to the dentist. I was forcing myself to keep the appointment.

The people at IBM looked spruce. The sales manager, whose name was Robert, was wearing a dark suit, a white shirt and a conservative tie. His assistant, Donna, was wearing the woman's equivalent—she looked like a successful young banker. They took me to a room where various demonstration units of word processors were on display. The units were as clean as Robert and Donna; I had seldom seen equipment so immaculate. My instinct was to make a run for it—get out while I still could. For one thing, I wasn't dressed well enough. My odd jacket and pants and blue shirt announced me as an infidel in the temple of business. Why hadn't I at least worn a suit for this first interview with the machine?

Robert sat me down among the glistening units. He would be glad to tell me, he said, all about the IBM "Displaywriter," as the company calls its word processing system. I looked around for the door. But the door was far away; there would be no tiptoeing back out now to the simple world of pencil and paper.

"The Displaywriter is designed to be user-friendly," Robert began. It was as good a way as any to begin; I certainly didn't want a machine that was user-hostile, or even user-indifferent. Robert said that the system was a good example of ergonomics—the science of trying to adapt working conditions to the worker. I hadn't ever heard of ergonomics, and even now it isn't a word I use every day. Still, it was comforting to know that such a concept exists in the workplace.

What I realized immediately was that the word processor wasn't just one piece of equipment. On the contrary, it had (as Robert explained) five separate components.

The first was a ninety-six-character keyboard of the kind

found on electric typewriters, only wider, with extended sides that contained a number of special keys marked DEL, MOVE, LINE ADJ, CHG FMT, GET, FIND, GO TO, PAGE END, REQST, PRINT, END, MSG, INDEX and CODE.

The second component was a terminal that looked like a TV screen. The screen, I was told, was big enough to accommodate twenty printed lines. This was important to me: a writer should always be able to see a good chunk of what he is writing.

The third unit was a large rectangular box, which the terminal was resting on. This was the electronics module, or, as Robert put it, the "brains of the typewriter." I said I was surprised that he called it a typewriter. "The system looks massive," he said, "but you've got to remember that it's just another typewriter." I said I'd try.

The fourth unit looked like a giant toaster. This was the diskette unit. Like any decent toaster, it had two slots. The slots were designed to hold two diskettes, or small disks. Diskettes contain the operating instructions that tell the entire system what to do; they also are the place where the words that are written on the screen get stored. They are, in short, the system's "software," as distinct from its "hardware." The hardware is exactly what its name suggests: the physical equipment that sits on the table, waiting to be used every day. It is, for instance, the keyboard and the screen and the toaster. The software is the infinitely variable set of programs, procedures and directions that can be put on a "floppy disk," or diskette, and that command the machine to execute the user's wishes. Unlike the pocket calculator and other simple computers, which perform their functions with their own internal hardware, the word processor can't operate without instructions from a separate diskette.

The fifth component—and the biggest of all—was a printer. The printer will type onto paper what the writer writes on the screen, word for word, page for page. It can't be operated manually; it responds solely to instructions from the mother unit. Nevertheless, despite its dependent status, it is an important member of the family, for without it all the words written on the terminal would exist only on the screen or on a diskette. The printer puts the words on good old-fashioned paper.

I was dismayed at the size of the system. For a man who doesn't like machines it was a lot of machinery. The very thought of trying to make all these different units work was intimidating. I wondered why the reporters I had seen at the *Times* and on *Lou Grant* weren't equally surrounded by bulky equipment. Robert explained what I should have guessed: that when a number of people are using computer terminals—at a newspaper, for instance, or in a business office—they can be connected to a central intelligence system. They can also share the same printer. But an individual writer using a word processor must have his own system of "brains" to activate his machine, his own "program" (the diskette) to tell it what to do, and his own printer to print what he writes.

"It's really very simple," Robert said. "Donna's going to demonstrate it for you."

Donna slid her typing chair over to what she called the keyboard module and put her beautifully manicured fingers on the keys. So far so good. She turned the power on with a switch, and the letters "IBM" loomed onto the terminal screen. The unit began to hum quietly.

"First you'll notice that none of these units is in a fixed position," Donna said. "That's one of the things we mean by ergonomics. You can rotate or tilt the screen to any angle that's comfortable for you. And you can move the keyboard away from the terminal; you can even put it on your lap. The diskette module can also be moved to another table, and the printer can be as far as two hundred feet away. So you've got some flexibility there. The whole system is adjustable to just about any kind of desk."

I thought that was very user-friendly.

"The color of the units is off-white," Donna went on, "because white is the easiest color for people to be around for a long period of time. The letters are green on a dark screen because our research has found that green is the least fatiguing to the eyes. But you've also got these knobs that will adjust the brightness and the contrast."

That also seemed ergonomical.

"Now you'll want to see how the equipment works," she said. "So what I'm going to do is load a program diskette into the diskette module." She inserted a disk into the first slot of the toaster. It made a series of clicking noises. "That's the sound of the program being loaded," she said. "You'll notice that it tells you what it's doing—right up here at the top of the screen. Everything above the green line is information for you. The rest of the screen is empty—that's your typing area."

On the space above the green line I saw the words PRO-GRAM LOADING—that was the machine telling me what it was doing—and a number of mysterious symbols: IAAGFA, Pg.1, Ln. 5, Kyb 1, Pitch 10. Then the clicking stopped, and the screen filled up with a long list of "tasks" that the machine was ready to perform, including create, revise, paginate, delete, duplicate, condense, erase, initialize, default and index. The program was obviously loaded.

I liked the idea of "create." But who could create on a monster like this? "Delete" and "erase" made me nervous, and "initialize" freaked me out; I would never master a system that asked me to initialize. The task that seemed to suit me best was "default." Whatever it meant, it was surely something I could do.

"This is your first menu," Donna explained, pointing to the list. "We call it a menu because it offers you a broad variety of choices. You have to choose one of these tasks to get started. Let's say you want to create a document."

"What does that mean?"

"It means you want to write something from scratch. So you press the letter that chooses TYPING TASKS. That's *a*." She pressed *a*. Nothing happened. "Then you have to press EN- TER," Donna said. "You always have to press ENTER." She pressed the ENTER key and a new menu appeared. It offered a choice of three typing tasks: create, revise or paginate.

"We want to create," she said, pressing the letter next to that item. Then she pressed ENTER again and the screen went blank. "There's your page—it's ready for whatever you want to write."

She started to type, copying a passage from a book, and typed several paragraphs on the "page." I tried to think of it as a page, but it still had the aura of an information bank; Donna could have been an airline clerk trying to get me a window seat in the nonsmoking section. Something about her didn't say "writer"—and it wasn't only that she was so well dressed. But then she began to demonstrate the word proc- essing functions that I had come to see, and I began to think of the sentences on the screen as real sentences—as actual writing.

"Suppose you want to delete this sentence," she said. "You simply press your DELETE button—like this—and the ma- chine asks you what you want to delete. See that message?" She pointed to the bottom of the screen, where two words had appeared: DELETE WHAT? Somehow I hadn't realized that the machine would have an identity of its own, that it would be able to talk back. I wasn't ready for that.

Donna had no such failure of nerve. Her fingers now sped over the keyboard as she demonstrated the machine's ability to delete, restore and insert. She moved words and clauses and whole paragraphs. The screen became a dancing sea of revisions and repairs. Long sentences suddenly vanished, but left no hole—the remaining sentences closed the gap and rearranged themselves as if nothing had been removed. Everything was instantly made tidy.

I tried to concentrate on what Donna was doing and what she was saying. Her words flew almost as fast as her fingers—strange words like "cursor" and "module" and "textpack," which were as familiar to her as "cat" and "dog," and maybe more familiar. My head swam; my palms sweated. Obviously the Displaywriter was a wonderful tool for editing and revising; just as obviously it was meant for a certain type of person, and that type of person was Donna.

"Now you try it," Donna said.

"Oh, no," I said. "I couldn't."

She got up and gave me her chair. "Sit right here," she said.

"Maybe I can come back next week," I said. I mumbled that I had to go.

"Just type something," she said.

I typed the usual something: "Now is the time for all good men to come to the aid of their party." Or maybe it was the one about the quick brown fox jumping over the lazy dog. I don't think I did "pack my box with five dozen liquor jugs," that printer's darling which uses all the letters of the alphabet more succinctly than any other phrase. It's just not something I say very often.

The touch of the keys was very easy, and the words

seemed to spring out of my fingers onto the screen. I was delighted and even a little surprised; I had assumed that only Donna's fingers would operate the machine. I typed on, writing a few sentences of my own. The good news was that the keys didn't "skip"—there were no spaces within the words. The bad news was that I made a lot of errors and couldn't get the hang of correcting them.

"You're very tense," Donna said. "Just relax." She was as soothing as a dental hygienist; in fact, I could have used a little mouthwash for dry-mouth syndrome. By now I had my coat off and my tie loosened and was beginning to look like a writer.

I typed a whole paragraph, and Donna explained how to delete and insert words and do a lot of other things like paginate and duplicate and store and retrieve. The deleting and inserting seemed quite simple, and I knew I could master them fairly soon. The other functions were more complex, and I took them on faith; I believed that the machine could do these various jobs. Whether I could also do them I didn't know.

But this was no time to quail. I had found out the main thing that I wanted to know: I could type on the keyboard and I could move the words on the screen. The rest would eventually get learned in one way or another.

I said that I was ready to take the plunge. Donna showed me how to "power down," and Robert and I turned our attention to contractual details. This was one area still untouched by new technology. The price lists and legal details were printed on paper, and so was the dotted line on which I was asked to sign—with a ballpoint pen—when the figures were all totted up.

I had three choices. I could buy the Displaywriter outright; I could rent it for six months at a substantial monthly rate; or I could lease it for three years at a lower rate. If I took the rental or the lease I would build an equity toward purchase.

I decided on the three-year lease and then watched in horror as Robert checked off six items: 192 K Byte Memory, Display Station, 96 Character K/Bd, Dual Diskette, 15 CPS Printer, and Textpack 1, which was the licensed program that I would get on my diskette. (It could have been worse: other licensed programs on the list were Asynchronous Communications, Bisynchronous Communications, and 3270 Data Stream Compatibility.) I had a choice of three printers and selected the least expensive one: it could only type 15½ characters per second; the other two were high-speed printers that could type 40 and 60 characters per second. As an extra option all three had an attachment that fed paper into the printer automatically. I skipped this option; I would feed my paper by hand.

Originally I had wanted to have my word processor at home. But the five units would take more space than I had anticipated, so I decided to put them in my office at the Book-of-the-Month Club. The idea made me self-conscious— learning a new skill is best done in privacy. But I also knew that I would master the equipment more quickly if it was near and if I got in the habit of using it routinely, like my typewriter, for whatever editorial jobs came along. I wanted to explore all the ways of making the equipment work both for myself and for the Club.

And so the contract was signed, the Rubicon crossed. That was in early December. Robert said that delivery would take about two weeks and that I should have my Displaywriter by the end of the year. I was hoping it would take longer. I should have felt a giddy sense of accomplishment as I walked back to my office. But I didn't. What I felt was that I had just bought a three-year lease on frustration and stress.

# 4. Four Hang-ups

My session with IBM gave me a lot to think about as I waited for my machine to arrive. I found myself thinking about some of the psychological blocks that people would bring to their first encounters with a word processor. Different blocks would be brought by different people, but all of them would be injurious and would have to be confronted and cleared away.

The hardest thing for me to think about was the idea of getting along without paper. The idea is alien to everything we know in our bones. People have been writing on paper, or papyrus, for four or five thousand years—long enough, anyway, to get into the habit. Paper is where we transact most of the routine business of life: letters, postcards, notes, lists, memos, bills, checks, receipts, notices, reminders to ourselves. Writing something on paper is one of the basic comforts. Even those of us who keep messy desks know that if we just burrow long enough in the piles of stuff we'll find the scrap of paper we're looking for—the one we didn't throw away because we knew that someday we might need it. The nightmare is to lose the crucial nugget of information: the recipe torn from a magazine, the name of the perfect little country inn, the phone number of a plumber who will come on Saturday.

Writers are unusually afraid of loss. The act of writing is so hard that just to get anything on paper is a small victory. A few terrible sentences are better than no sentences at all; they may at least contain a thought worth saving, a phrase that can be reshaped. The important thing is that these fragments exist somewhere in the physical world. The paper that they're written on can be held, stared at, marked up, put aside and reexamined later. Ten or twenty pages can be spread out on the floor and rearranged with scissors and paste. Scissors and paste are honorable writers' tools. So is the floor.

I could hardly imagine throwing all this away—not only the paper itself, but the security blanket. With my new word processor I would type my words and see them materialize on a screen. At that moment the words would, I suppose, exist. But would they *really* exist? Not in any sense that I had ever thought of words before. They would be mere shadows of light. If I pressed the wrong key, couldn't they just vanish into thin air? (No air is thinner than the air into which a writer starting out on a word processor thinks his words will vanish.) Or even if I pressed the right key and stored my words correctly overnight on a disk, would I be able to call them back in the morning? Would I ever see them again? The chances of my never seeing them again struck me as high. I didn't trust what I couldn't hold. Paper was the one reality in writing.

That was my first block. I wondered how I would get past it—and if I would.

The second block was what I'll call the humanist hang-up. This is the snobbery of liberal-arts types who don't understand science or technology and don't want to. It's a group that I belong to myself, so I know its biases and phobias. Our unifying belief is that science has somehow been the cause of everything that has messed up the world and made it so complex and impersonal. If it would just go away. If we could just be left to our exquisitely sensitive appreciation of art and music and literature, of history and philosophy and the classics—the really civilized fields.

Perhaps we aren't snobs so much as we are cowards. We're afraid of how stupid we feel in the presence of science, and so we take refuge in feeling superior. We have never had an aptitude for math or chemistry or engineering, and we are fearful that we won't understand what we read and hear every day about quantum physics, or solid state electronics, or gene splicing, or quasars and quarks. These are mysteries too arcane for us dummies to fathom. Better not to try.

But what really makes us dummies is that we give up so easily. I often think of the pleasure I've lost by shying away from fields that I thought would be too hard to grasp. Only in recent years have I started to glimpse the elegance of the physical and mathematical world by reading the work of scientists who also were writers—men and women like Rachel Carson, Lewis Thomas, Margaret Mead, René Dubos, Jeremy Bernstein and Loren Eiseley. They seem to me to be the true humanists. I envy them their gift for seeing the world whole and not in isolated parts.

Most of us who are afraid of science are also uncomfortable with machines. As a boy I was never taught to tinker and to fix things, and as a man I have lived in a society of servicemen who will repair what has gone wrong. When a piece of machinery breaks, my instinct has always been to hit it, or to yank at it—to force it, somehow, to lurch back into action. It's the blind instinct of a man who regards machines as his enemy. Only later does it occur to me that the broken gadget was built to operate by a series of logical steps and that I might locate the problem by tracing those steps. Even then the idea that I might be able to fix it is almost inconceivable, and when I occasionally succeed I tend to think it was mostly luck.

It's not that I disapprove of technology. On the contrary, I'm grateful for its blessings. I love to drive a car, though I have only a vague notion of what is under the hood or how the combustion engine works. I love to fly in a plane, though I'm fuzzy about the law of aerodynamics that holds such an immense object up in the sky. Surely it defies that other law (which I also hope nobody asks me to explain)—the law of gravity. I'm a fan of the electric light, but my knowledge of the ohm is limited to crossword puzzles—and that goes for the erg and the ampere and the watt.

The point is that it's not necessary to understand the wonders of technology in order to enjoy them, and this should be as true of computers as it is of cars. Yet there is no end of grumbling about them. "I don't want to have anything to do with computers," I keep hearing people say. I used to say it myself, and part of me still continued to think it.

That was obviously a hang-up.

The third block is the exact opposite of the one I have just described. It belongs to all the people who are not liberal-arts types—people whose bent is for science and technology and commerce and industry. Their block is that they don't think they have to bother to learn how to write clear English. At the IBM showroom I had seen enough of the word processor to suspect that it could greatly help people to clean up their sentences by focusing their mind on the act of writing and revising. But over the years I had also seen enough writing by America's technical and business people to feel that they are almost beyond salvation.

Here is a typical example of how corporate America conducts its daily business in memos:

> Product usability objective setting should be a direct outgrowth of the initial opportunity definition of your program, plus the specific usability oriented information gathered during priority setting and the requirements definition activity.

It's little short of criminal to inflict such a memo on a group of employees or colleagues. How much energy do Americans expend every day trying to figure out what people in authority are trying to say? How many good ideas are lost in the murk of Memoville? How many official explanations totally fail to explain? Consider how the airlines tell their passengers—in a notice stapled to every ticket—what to expect if a flight is overbooked:

> OVERBOOKING OF FLIGHTS
> If there are not enough volunteers the airline will deny boarding to other persons in accordance with its particular boarding priority.

This kind of writing is endemic to American life. Much of what is disseminated by businesses, banks, insurance companies, manufacturers, technical firms, government agencies, educational systems and health institutions—both internally and to the public—is as hard to decipher as an ancient rune, and a great deal of it makes no sense at all. This is because the people who are doing the writing don't stop to think that this is in fact what they are doing. Writing is something that "writers" do.

But writers are only a fraction of the population. The rest

of the citizens are in some other line of work, and vast numbers of them write something during the day that gets foisted on other people. Yet very few people realize how badly they write and how badly this hurts them and their career and their company. People are judged on the basis of who they appear to be in their writing, and if what they write is pompous or fuzzy or disorganized they will be perceived as all those things. Bad writing makes bright people look dumb.

How did we get into this fix? It's the humanist hang-up in reverse. People who never had a knack for words usually hated English when they were in school and stopped taking it as soon as they could. Now, out in the world where they need to write, they are as afraid of writing as I am afraid of science. They have writing anxiety. They don't know how to start.

One way to start is to realize that writing is a craft, like carpentry or cabinetmaking, with its own set of tools, which are words. Writing is not some sort of divine act that can only be performed by people of artistic bent, though obviously a gift for words is helpful. Writing is the logical arrangement of thought. Anybody who thinks clearly should be able to write clearly—if he learns how to use the tools. Anybody whose thinking is muddy will never write clearly.

To clarify what we write, it is important to see what we are writing and to constantly ask, "Have I said what I wanted to say?" Usually we haven't. Even for a professional writer very few sentences come out right the first time, or even the second or third time. Almost every sentence has some flaw: it's not clear; it could mean several different things; it's not logical; it's cluttered with unnecessary words or phrases; it has too many words that are long and lifeless; it's pretentious; it lacks rhythm.

These are problems that a writer systematically attacks.

Like a watchmaker or any other artisan, he wants to build something that works as simply and as smoothly as possible— with no extra parts to get in the way—and he fiddles with his materials until they are right. Nonwriters don't do this. Nobody has told them that rewriting is the essence of writing—that their first draft is probably poor and that they have a second and a third chance to make it better. The worst offenders tend to be bosses who dictate to a secretary. Most people's spoken sentences are full of repetition and disarray. Therefore the man who dictates should see what he has said after it has been typed. One of the things he will see is that he could have said it in half the number of words.

Seeing is a key to writing. What the word processor could do is to revolutionize the way we think about words by displaying them for our consideration and giving us an instant chance to reconsider them. It will also draw far more people into the act of writing. In a few years, professional men and women in every field and at every level will be writing on word processors to conduct their daily business. I hope that as their words appear on the terminal screen they will begin to see them as tools that they can use like any other tools— without fear, and maybe even with pleasure.

The fourth block is the typing block.

A word processor has the same basic keyboard as a typewriter; therefore anyone who uses it must know how to type. But a surprising number of otherwise competent professional people—especially men—have never learned this fundamental skill. For many men it's a sexist hang-up: typing is something women do. It's all right for men to type if they are writers; their image has been validated by macho authors like Hemingway and by movies about tough reporters in snap-brim hats. But for a man with executive ambitions to sit down at a typewriter and bang out a memo or a letter is an indignity. Better to have Miss Smithers ("a really wonderful gal") do it, even if she can't get to it until tomorrow.

What is lost, among other things, is independence. A person who can type is a person in control of an important area of his life: how he communicates with other people. Most writers, for instance, type their own letters—it's quick, and the writing is warm and direct. I would hate to filter what I say through Miss Smithers, wonderful though she is. What I type is who I am. When a secretary is brought into the act, writing stiffens and loses its spontaneity.

These, of course, are subjective reasons, related to my feelings about the writing process and about the role of women in America's offices. But there is a practical reason that is far more compelling. With the advent of computers it will be crucial for managers and other people who work in offices to have "keyboard skills."

"Suppose a manager must get in touch with the London or San Francisco office," said a recent piece in *The New York Times* analyzing the office of the future. "To operate at maximum efficiency he or she will not interrupt a secretary for a quick memo but will sit down at the keyboard and type. During a typical day a business manager might use terminals several times to write memos to out-of-town offices. Productivity is the key."

Nor will there be as many secretaries to interrupt. "The number of young, semi-skilled people for clerical jobs continues to decline," the *Times* noted. "This means that there will be more direct-support computers for managers who do not have enough people support. Middle management officers will certainly be typing."

Ironically, many bright and educated young women have avoided learning how to type—or admitting that they already know how—because they have seen how often this skill gets them deflected from a possible good job into one that is clerical and demeaning. The word processor could be the answer to everybody's problem because it isn't stereotyped by sex. Although it's just a glorified typewriter, it doesn't look like a typewriter. It's modern and sleek. You'd almost expect to see it on the command deck of the starship *Enterprise*. A woman can sit at its keyboard and not be taken for a secretary. So can a man.

Anybody can learn to type. It's one of those skills that become habitual with practice, like driving a car. If typing is your block, invest in a typing course. Don't get stuck with the hang-ups of today when everyone else is flourishing in the office of tomorrow.

# 5.   It Arrives

A few days before Christmas a package was delivered to my office. By its size and shape it looked as if it contained two or maybe three bottles of bourbon. It also weighed that much—about eight pounds—when I picked it up. I hadn't been expecting any such Christmas cheer, and, as it turned out when I saw the label, I wasn't getting any. The label said "IBM" and the contents were listed as "instructional materials." Eight pounds of instructional materials! I put the box in a far corner of my office and tried not to look at it. Soon enough I would have to poke into its dreary innards. There was no need to spoil the holidays.

Robert had assured me that IBM would provide "support help" when my machine was installed. Someone would come over and give me a lesson. He also said that the company had a hotline in Dallas with an 800 telephone number; experts were standing by, twenty-four hours a day, to help me in my times of need. I knew how that worked: I had seen plenty of aviation movies in which the control tower—usually in Wichita—talks the crippled airliner down when the captain and the copilot are dead. ("Listen carefully, Debbie—do you see a little red button and next to it a knob that

says 'altitude'? Good. Now what I want you to do . . .") I
pictured myself on the phone to kindly technicians in Dallas
who would coax me through the long descent from anxiety
to calm.

But Robert had also warned me not to become dependent.
"Our instruction books are written so that in theory you
should be able to teach yourself," he said. That was one theory I had no reason to believe in. Instructional prose is one of
the most forbidding swamps in the whole realm of language.

Christmas came and went. The days were dwindling
down. Then, on the last day of December, *it* arrived. Five
big cartons were carried into my office and piled next to my
desk. They dominated the room, crowding me with their
presence. Every time I looked at them I felt a knot in my
stomach. I tried to ignore them. I typed some letters on my
Underwood and saw the old year and the old technology out.

On the first Monday of the new year I opened the five
cartons and removed the five units. With a little help from
my friends I connected the various electrical cables and
plugged them in. No adapters to provide extra voltage were
necessary; presumably the word processor doesn't use any
more current than a Cuisinart.

I put the four main units—keyboard, screen, electronic
module and toaster—on a table just behind my desk, where I
could get at them easily, and pushed my typewriter farther
away. Next to the glossy newcomers it looked like an object
in the Smithsonian. I put the printer on a table in a far corner of the room, stringing its cable across the rug. This eased
the congestion—the printer is the biggest of the five units—
and it also eased the psychological assault.

Still, I found it hard to believe that I had brought into my
life a set of writing devices that I would always have to activate. I couldn't just sit down and write; I would have to think

about pushing certain keys and inserting certain diskettes.
Now, just to push the ON switch seemed like a major decision.
Not at all to my surprise, I kept putting it off.

Finally, late in the afternoon, I opened the box of instructional materials. They consisted of three huge looseleaf book-
lets: "Operator Training, Book 1—Basic Topics"; "Operator
Training, Book 2—Selectable Topics"; and "Operator Reference Package." A note at the beginning of Book 1 explained:
"This is a major revision of, and obsoletes, S-544-0863." I had
never seen the verb "to obsolete" before and never wanted to
see it again. If this was typical of the English that IBM would
be using to shepherd me into the world of tomorrow I might
take a long time getting there.

Another note on the same page announced that "this
equipment generates, uses and can radiate radio frequency
energy that may cause interference in a residential area," in
which case "the user at his own expense will be required to
take whatever measures may be required to correct the interference." That certainly obsoleted my typewriter—the
neighbors never complained about it once.

I turned to page 1. It said: "Your training begins in this
book, Book 1. You should complete Book 1. Read every page
unless otherwise directed, and follow the directions carefully-
ly." Something about the tone took me back to grammar
school; I caught a whiff of chalk in the air and heard Mr.
Spicer grilling me on the multiplication table.

The next paragraph said that if I didn't understand any of
the "training materials" I could call the IBM Office Systems
Support Center. "Center personnel will answer your questions," it said, "and direct you to additional support, if appropriate." That was the catch: "if appropriate." Would support for me be deemed appropriate? Would *I* be deemed
appropriate? One thing was certain—I'd better not call the

Center personnel before I consulted the Office Systems Support Center Guide and tried to find the solution myself. The book made that very clear.

Following directions, I switched the power to ON. That went very well: the screen lit up and the machine began to hum.

I took the program diskette out and put it in the left slot of the diskette unit (the toaster). The unit made a series of clunking noises that startled me; had I done something wrong already? Fortunately, the clunking was normal—it was just the sound of the program loading itself into the system. This must be done every time the power is turned on: the program is what gives the machine its instructions. Every time the power is turned off, the program is cleared from the system.

When the program was loaded, my first "menu" appeared on the screen. A menu is a list of different tasks that the machine will perform. Each task has an identifying letter: $a$, $b$, $c$, $d$, etc.

The first item on the first menu ($a$) refers to TYPING TASKS, a general category that includes three specific typing tasks: creating a document, revising a document, and paginating a document. The letter $b$ refers to WORK DISKETTE TASKS, which include such functions as duplicating or erasing or naming a work diskette, and $c$ refers to PROGRAM DISKETTE TASKS, which include changing the instructions on the program diskette.

To do any of these jobs you must make a choice that will take you from this general menu to one that is more specific. If you want to do a typing task, for instance, you press the letter $a$, and then press ENTER. This brings onto the screen a more specific menu, which enables you to select one of the three typing tasks.

On this second menu the letter $a$, for instance, means CRE-

ATE DOCUMENT. By pressing that letter you get a blank screen and can start to write. By pressing *b*, or REVISE DOCUMENT, you summon to the screen something that you have already written and that you want to revise or continue. The larger point is that the system always takes you in successive steps to the stage you want to reach, giving you various chances along the way to change the format or make some other alteration.

Now it may seem that this larger point—this sequential process that I assume is fundamental to all computers—was clear to me right away. It wasn't. Only after plodding slowly through the training book, with many false starts and moments of despair, did I begin to glimpse what the machine was driving at and how it tended to "think." From the very beginning I felt inferior. The machine just seemed enormously complex.

One reason, of course, was its sheer size: five big and bulky units. But two other reasons occurred to me.

The first was terminology. I had plunged headlong into a new world which, like any specialized field, had its own vocabulary. The words were strange. Diskette. Program diskette. Work diskette. Work station. Default. Condense. Initialize. They jumped out of the screen and out of the instruction manuals, clogging and clouding the brain.

Some, though genteel, were relatively easy. A diskette, for instance, was just a disk. But which kind of diskette was which? What exactly was the difference between the "program diskette" and the "work diskette"? Surely some kind of "work" got done on the program diskette. And where was the "work station" that the menu kept inviting me to use? I didn't remember unpacking it.

As it turned out, the work station is the printer and the table that it sits on. As for the work diskette, it's the diskette

that I'm supposed to put into the "diskette unit" (the toaster)
to store my own work on. It's a blank disk that I can buy at a
store, like a blank tape for a tape recorder. The program
diskette is the disk that IBM does *its* work on; it's patented,
and I can't buy it at any store. In short, the work diskette is
my disk and the program diskette is their disk.

Such things gradually become clear. The moral is: Don't
be panicked by the ornate words. Relax and try to figure out
what they mean in everyday English. When a work station
becomes a mere printer it loses much of its mystery.

The other reason for the complexity is that the machine is
throwing at the beginner far more than he initially needs to
know. This is inevitable. The word processor, after all, has
been designed to process letters and numbers in all the ways
in which people arrange them—in arithmetical tables, in
aligned columns, in footnotes—and then to print them in all
the ways that people want their documents printed. If it
didn't meet the countless special needs of the modern office
it wouldn't be a useful product and nobody would buy it.

But this means that it presents a formidable face to the
user. Every menu that appears on the terminal says: "Look
what I can do! I can index! I can paginate! I can copy! I can
file! I can recover documents! I can spell! I can print!" And
there's no relief in fleeing to the instruction books. There the
system becomes positively feverish with pride: "I can do sta-
tistics! I can prehyphenate! I can do multi-page documents
and personalized alternate formats! I can assemble repetitive
paragraphs and insert variable information! I can do columns
with flush right margins! I can keep tables from splitting
during pagination! I can do Roman numerals with indented
paragraphs! I can print a letter with blind carbon copies and
envelopes. You want bibliographies? You've got 'em. Footnotes? Superscripts? Why not? Supplemental dictionaries?
No problem."

It's too much. My brain reeled at the sight of all those intricate functions that I would never master. Everything that I had feared was coming true: I really was too dumb for the machine. I felt paralyzed and didn't want to keep going.

Then, one day, I had a brilliant thought. I didn't *need* to master all those functions. I only wanted to do some writing. And some rewriting. And some printing. And maybe a little pagination. Let other persons personalize alternate formats and insert variable information. Let table-keepers keep tables and keep them from splitting. I would learn what I needed to know. If the day should come when I absolutely had to assemble some repetitive paragraphs I could probably do it. Anybody can do anything if he wants to do it badly enough.

This was a liberating idea, and it helped me to get through the first weeks. When the instruction book led me down trails that I didn't think I would ever want to follow, I just hurried over them until I came to friendlier terrain. I knew this would horrify the people who wrote the book; they make a big deal about not proceeding to Topic B until you have completed Topic A and have also done the question-and-answer review. The punitive aura of the schoolroom is never far away; in fact, I was sure that the machine *knew* I had skipped certain sections and had only pretended to have studied them. No wonder the dream of being unprepared for an exam recurs throughout our lives—guilt is the companion of homework from childhood on. The IBM people were making me feel guilty now. But that still didn't mean I was going to do all their terrible lessons.

The best system of learning to write on a word processor will involve some combination of self-instruction and personal coaching. Today many organizations offer seminars for people who are starting out on a computer or for managers who should at least know how computers operate. Companies like IBM that manufacture and sell the equipment usually provide some indoctrination and follow-up support. Certainly any firm that converts its office to word processors should give its employees a brief course in how to use them. There's no substitute for having a real person explain how a new and baffling machine works. Trying to learn solely from a book is too lonely and frustrating.

I found this out very soon. The instruction book called "Basic Topics" is a step-by-step course that is meant to be studied in conjunction with a "training diskette." In other words, instead of loading the toaster with a work diskette of my own, I loaded it with IBM's training diskette. This took me through all the basic procedures by giving me instructions on the screen. It gave me lessons in how to load a diskette, how to select different tasks from a menu, how to use the cursor, how to use such keys as DELETE, MOVE and FIND, how to duplicate a document, how to print, and other basic functions. It was a good method, and I learned a lot.

But still many points were not clear. Sometimes, for instance, the training diskette told me that I would see something on the screen which in fact did not appear. Occasionally I also found that a crucial step in a sequential process was missing—I didn't get a command from the book or the diskette that I thought I needed. Whether these failures were my fault or IBM's I never knew. I tended to blame myself.

That's who the machine also tended to blame. It wrote me dozens of messages in our first days together. Most of them explained what I should do next and were therefore helpful. But I also got a dismaying number of messages that told me I had done something wrong. INVALID KEY was one of the machine's favorites. I seemed to hit a great many invalid keys, though I never knew what invalidated them. WRONG DISKETTE, the machine would say, without telling me what was wrong with it or which diskette would be right. REMOVE PA-PER JAM FROM PRINTER, it would say, knowing long before I did that I had jammed my paper. DOCUMENT NEEDS RECOV-ERY, it would say, telling me what I most didn't want to hear—that whatever I was working on had somehow vanished. Where? How? DISKETTE IS UNSUPPORTED DISKETTE TYPE; PRINT JOB CANCELLED, it would say, lashing me with both crime and punishment. I was made to feel that I was putting the machine to a lot of trouble. What it conveyed was: "You really screwed up but I'll try my best." I expected to see a message that said YOU DUMMY! or NOT AGAIN! What I wanted the machine to say was HEY YOU'RE TERRIFIC! or YOU'RE REALLY A SWELL GUY ANYWAY. It never did.

After a week I had a lot of questions that needed answering. I also needed human contact. I called Robert at IBM and asked what kind of help I was entitled to. He said that the systems engineer assigned to my territory would come over and give me a lesson in the morning. He said her name was Barbara.

I instantly felt better. Barbara was coming. Barbara would make everything all right. Barbara would answer all my questions and also tell me how terrific I was. Barbara would make me feel less alone.

In the morning I was as fidgety as a teen-ager waiting for an important date. I had never had a date with a systems engineer. Barbara arrived punctually at ten. She didn't look like a systems engineer. I welcomed her as if she were arriving at the train station for the big football weekend. She must have been astonished at how glad I was to see her.

She took off her coat and pulled up a chair next to mine at the Displaywriter. As she sat there beside me, ready to impart her sacred mysteries, she seemed to have come from some remote pedagogical corner of my past. The piano teacher? No, someone more piquant. The memory diskette in my head called back a moment in my adolescence when my mother gave me dance lessons at Arthur Murray's—one of her periodic attempts to make me more debonair. Miss Vernon and I went round and round in a mirrored room, prisoners of the notion that every male can learn to tango. Now Barbara and I were met on equally uncertain ground.

I showed her some of the things I had learned to do on the keyboard and asked her all the questions I had written in preparation for her visit. Why does *this* happen? What does it mean when the screen says *that?* How can I get from here to here? The book says X but I always get Y. Why does it keep saying REQUIRED CARRIER RETURN up there at the top? I don't understand how to make this work for instance if I'm trying to begin a new paragraph on this line down here and the cursor is over there and the message tells me that the program diskette in the left slot won't . . .

I kept apologizing for wanting points explained that were surely obvious. But Barbara was supportive. She told me what any student wants to know—that I was making good progress and that it was hard for everybody at first and that I shouldn't be discouraged—and she clarified all the problems that I hadn't been able to solve.

She asked if I had defaulted my program diskette yet, and I said I hadn't. In fact, that whole procedure had seemed so complex that I was intending to save it for Barbara's second visit. Would I like her to default it for me now? Would I!

"Default" is IBM's unlikely word for the process of tailoring your program diskette to your individual needs or whims. I told Barbara, for instance, that as a writer I would always want the printer to double-space my copy. (Writers and editors hate single-spaced copy.) I also told her how wide I wanted my margins and where I always wanted the printer to type the first line—five lines from the top of the page.

Barbara "defaulted" my program diskette accordingly by giving the machine these instructions on the menu called "Program Diskette Tasks." If I ever wanted to change the format I could. Meanwhile I would be spared the trouble of instructing the machine each time I started to write. Other people would want different defaults: special tab settings, for example. Or they might want to have the pages numbered in a certain way. Later I would want other defaults myself. For now I was just glad that when the time came for me to print my copy it would look reasonably familiar.

My lesson ended and I felt much better. Barbara was not only a good teacher who knew her technology and knew how to explain it. She also understood the larger purpose that I had in mind—using the word processor to write a book. I was glad to have found a friend I could call on with all the technical and emotional problems that were bound to arise in the weeks ahead.

I asked Barbara when she would be coming again.

"There's something I have to tell you," she said.

I've heard that phrase often enough—in life and in the movies—to know that it never augurs anything good.

"Our division is being reorganized," Barbara said. "I've been assigned to a new district. I won't be able to see you again."

"But we were just . . ."

"I only heard about it this morning," she said. "There's nothing I can do."

Barbara saw how upset I was. She was a sensitive systems engineer.

"Look," she said, "they'll assign someone else to my territory in a few weeks when things get straightened out."

I wasn't consoled.

"Besides, I want you to start using our hotline telephone. Those people out in Dallas can help you just as much as I can."

I wanted to tell her that it wouldn't be the same. It takes two to tango. But she was gone. She gave me a firm handshake and wished me luck and walked out of my life.

# 6. Eyestrain

One thing that I noticed after only a week of training was that my eyes were very tired. I had partly expected this; friends on newspapers had mentioned that they felt a certain amount of eyestrain after a day_of editing copy on a terminal. But that was a whole day. My eyes were tired after only half an hour. And it was the kind of eye fatigue that saps the whole metabolism. I didn't want to do anything that involved keeping my eyes open. What I mostly wanted to do was sleep.

This was a real setback. Had I come this far—emotionally and financially—just to find that I was physically unsuited to writing at a terminal?

I discussed my troubles with anyone who would listen and soon identified the main villains as brightness and glare. The problem lies in the fact that what we read on a terminal screen is not black type on white paper. It's just the opposite: we are reading light surrounded by black. This is a new experience for the eye. Literate man has always wanted enough light to read by. Now it turns out that enough is too much.

Someone pointed out to me that the fluorescent bulbs in

the ceiling of my office were very bright: just turning on my overhead lights made me squint. I reduced their wattage by half and also had a grid put on them that reduced their glare. The room immediately became far more comfortable, and the words on my terminal screen were clearer and easier to read.

But I continued to see several kinds of light in my screen. One was the reflection of my desk light: a bright blob in the middle of what I was trying to read. There was also a great deal of daylight reflected onto the screen from the nearby window.

Having finally noticed these obvious phenomena, I didn't have to be Thomas Edison to think of a solution. After that, whenever I used the word processor I turned off my desk light and pulled the window shades.

My eyes felt better right away. I was still conscious of eye fatigue when I used the machine for any length of time, but at least it was no longer a crippling ailment.

Various other possible refinements occurred to me. I found out, for instance, that some computer firms sell glare filters and colored gels that can be attached to a terminal screen. One person's restful green might be someone else's restful red. My ophthalmologist, who has reattached thousands of retinas, including mine, tells me that different colors are processed by different cones of the retina. It's conceivable, he says, that a writer using a word processor for many hours could get relief by periodically changing colors. I offer this for whatever it's worth, and if it's worth anything the royalties should go to him.

A small body of alarmist literature has bobbed up since America's writing went electronic, alleging that newspaper reporters and editors who work all day at terminals run a long-term risk of getting cataracts. There appears to be no medical evidence to support this charge. Parents whose children use computers in the classroom have also had studies made and have concluded that there is apparently no danger.

The main problem will continue to be eye fatigue. People accustomed to the printed page will probably always notice a certain weariness setting in when they write on a word processor. The new technology is only partly to blame. My doctor says that anything will make your eyes tired if you look at it long enough. One lesson for the writer would therefore seem to be: Don't look at the words on the screen any more than you need to. Look down at the keyboard, or stare into space, while you're waiting for the next sentence to form.

As any writer will testify, this can be one of life's longest intervals. In fact, if you put all these intervals together you may give your eyes more rest than they need.

# 7.  Privacy

Another novelty that I hadn't expected is that the word processor makes writing a public act. Like all writers, I'm self-conscious about the words that I put on paper and I don't want anybody else to see them until I think they're right. (Then, like all writers, I can't wait to see them in print and to have everybody else see them.) In this miserable state the writer has always been protected by social codes governing behavior. It's just not polite—so we are instructed at an early age—to look over someone's shoulder when he or she is writing by hand or at a typewriter. The committing of thoughts to paper is a deed that by civilized consent we are allowed to do alone.

No such constraints apply to writing done on a terminal screen. I had no sooner started to work at my word processor, tentatively pecking out sentences and shyly experimenting with the various special keys, than I discovered that I was performing a spectator sport. People were standing behind me looking at the screen. They gave every appearance of being fascinated by what I was causing to happen.

Quite a few were interested in the color of the letters. Some of them said they thought the green words were pretty; some said they would never be able to write with green words. Some were surprised that the letters were so big and easy to read; some were surprised that the words were so small and hard to read. Some just stood and watched, like barflies watching a baseball game. Some said that *they* would never be caught dead writing on a contraption like that. Some were obviously eager to have me finish a sentence I had begun—the TV watcher's God-given right is to know how the story comes out.

It didn't occur to any of them that they were intruding, and I realized that the odd one in the room, for even thinking such a thought, was me. We have become a society of television viewers, and the screen belongs to everyone. It's not protected by the First Amendment, or by any other amendment, or by Emily Post. Any American can go into a mall and watch any other American play a video game. I was an American playing a video game. I was not a writer except in my own tired eyes; nobody else who saw me at my keyboard perceived me as a writer.

Maybe this is just as well. Maybe writers have coddled themselves too long with the notion that they can only tend their holy flame in holy solitude. Maybe they're tougher than they think. Maybe the screen will loosen as many writers' blocks as it tightens. Who knows? Not me. All I can tell you is that you're in for some surprises as you hunch over your keyboard in the agony of creation, imagining yourself alone with the silken phrases that you are spinning, spider-like, out of your innards.

My advice is simple: Don't look around.

# 8.    The Day It Happened

I knew that sooner or later the dreaded day would come
when something I wrote got lost. The day came sooner.

I had finished my training in the "Basic Topics" instruction book. I had done various other exercises of my own de-
vising—copying passages out of books, playing with the
words on the screen, trying to get the hang of the printer.
Barbara had come and Barbara had gone. I was on my own.

I was still very neurotic about the machine. It continued to
intimidate me just by the fact that it was a machine. I didn't
turn to it with any ease; on the contrary, I gave concerted
thought to every step—even to minor steps that should have
become routine. I was afraid that if I pushed the wrong key I
would cause some disaster I couldn't reverse.

Finally I decided that if I was going to do my own writing
on the machine I should do it. My training was over; I would
start writing my book—this book.

I put a new work diskette in my diskette unit, and when
the screen asked me to name the "document" I named it
PROCESS because it was going to be a book about writing on a
word processor. The machine accepted the name—it didn't
say "That's a dumb name for a document"—and I was
launched. All I had to do was write.

I pressed enough keys to get me through all the menus until the screen gave me a blank "page." Then, with the enormous confidence of a writer who knows exactly what he wants to say, I typed "Chapter One." The wonderful words appeared on the screen, nicely centered. (I had nicely centered them.) I felt pretty good.

I had given some thought to how I wanted to begin, so I started right in. Real sentences began to appear on the screen, one after another. Then I had a real paragraph. Then I started another paragraph. Soon I had a second paragraph. I was *writing!* To my surprise, it seemed quite natural. I had somehow supposed that I would have to think differently about the process of putting words together—that the screen would alter instincts and reflexes that were deeply ingrained. But there was no difference. The sentences on the screen were mine—I recognized the style. The machine had not made them mechanical.

And that wasn't all. Two other features struck me as vastly pleasurable.

One was the touch of the keys. I could hardly believe how quickly and easily and silently I typed as my writing gathered momentum. The physical labor of pounding on a typewriter was gone; the weight of a lifetime was lifted from my fingers and shoulders. My words leaped instantly onto the screen—and instantly off again when I changed or erased them.

The other incredible thing was that I didn't have to use a carriage return; the machine performed that task for me. When a word was too long to fit at the end of a line it simply moved itself down to the next line. (The diskette could also have been programmed to hyphenate.) I found this very liberating. My inner ear no longer listened for the warning bell that signified the end of the line; I no longer had to break my writing rhythm to swing the carriage back by hand. In

theory I could type one line into eternity and it would arrange itself into an endless series of lines and paragraphs and
pages. Nirvana! Technology was my buddy after all.

I wrote with enjoyment for about an hour. I said some
things that I wanted to say, and with the DELETE button I
removed some things that I realized I didn't want to say, and
I had the satisfaction of knowing that what I had written was
something I could use.

Suddenly a string of digits and letters appeared at the bottom of my screen, stretching across its entire width: 900-FFFA-
OEll-4C00-00-OBl4-06AE-0B92-28-lAAGFA. It was a terrible sight. I
hated all the numbers, but the only three that I cared about
were the first three: 900. When an IBM message begins with
900 it means that something is wrong with some part of the
equipment.

Naturally I assumed that it was my fault. I had inadvertently pressed a key that had caused some wires to cross, or
even to melt. Soon I could expect to see smoke. I tried to
move the cursor, but it wouldn't move. I pressed the keys
like END that would store on my diskette everything I had
written up to that point. Nothing happened. I realized with
horror that 900 takes priority over all other moves. Thou shalt
not continue, it says, until the equipment is fixed.

I left the power on and telephoned the hotline in Dallas. I
was surprised at how agitated I was: hands clammy, pulse a
little up. It was the first time I had felt what it was like to
have written something I might not be able to retrieve. What
I had written was probably no great shakes, and maybe no
shakes at all. But at this moment it loomed as a jewel of
prose—sensitive, witty, wise. I couldn't stand the thought of
losing it.

The man who answered the hotline in Dallas was cool. I
started to blurt out my symptoms, but he only wanted some

numbers: my "access code" and my "900" digits. Just like a doctor, I thought—all business, no sympathy.

"I'm going to turn you over to one of our systems analysts," he said, and I was put on Hold. In the background I heard recorded music. It was a samba, strenuously peppy— piped in, presumably, from a Texas radio station. I resented the music; my machine was about to explode and I had to sit and listen to a samba.

I waited fifteen minutes. Finally an operator came on and said that all the lines were still busy. Did I want to call back?

"No," I snapped. "I'll wait. I've already been waiting fifteen minutes."

"That's odd," she said. "My terminal shows you've only been waiting four minutes." Another nut, she was saying to herself.

She took pity and put me through to a systems support person. "Hello, Mr. Zinsser. This is Kathy. May I help you?"

Oh sweet Texas angel, let me tell you my troubles. I was just typing along, minding my own business, when suddenly . . . and I poured out the whole story.

Kathy tried to calm me down. She asked me to read her my 900 number, and I did—all thirty-seven digits and letters. That made me feel better. At least she knew the facts, for better or for worse. Now she just had to make a diagnosis. I could almost hear her stroking her chin in Hippocratic meditation.

Finally she said, "Hmmmm." I took it to be the "Hmmmm" of a doctor looking at X-rays and seeing more than he wanted to see.

"I don't recognize that code," Kathy said. "It's a very unusual complaint—something wrong with your software. I'm going to call our experts in Austin and I'll call you right back. Don't go away."

I hung up the phone and sat staring at my sick machine. It had swallowed my words and gone into shock. What would the Austin people say? Why didn't Kathy call back? I thought of all the occasions when I have waited for a doctor to call back. There is no longer unit of time.

The minutes inched by. The phone rang and I grabbed it. It was Kathy. "What's wrong?" I said.

"Austin checked its records," Kathy said, "and they found that some other customers have had trouble with that particular program diskette. It doesn't happen often, but I guess it just happened to you."

"I guess it did."

"Well, anyway, our later diskettes don't have that problem, so we'll send you one of the new ones."

"Yes, but . . . "

"Meanwhile you'll have to turn the power off in order to get started again."

That was the worst thing she could have said. Any novice knows that you don't turn the power off until you've stored your material on the work diskette.

"But Kathy . . ."

"Turn it off. Then we'll see after that if we can recover your document."

I switched the machine off. It went dead—no light, no sound. I didn't feel so good myself.

"Now turn it on again," Kathy said, "and let's try to recover your document." She put me through an elaborate drill, telling me to press various unmarked keys, their function known only to her.

"What do you see?" she asked.

"Nothing," I said. I have never seen more nothing than what wasn't on my screen.

"Well, then," she said, "I'm afraid you'll just have to retype what you did this morning."

"From what?"

"Well, I assume you were working from out of a book or something."

"I was working from out of my head," I said. I realized that I was yelling into the phone. I was also in a cold sweat.

"You mean you were *writing* something," Kathy said.

"Yes."

There was a long pause. Finally I was the one who continued the conversation. "What happened?" I asked.

"Well," she said, "your stuff was just out in the electricity and it's gone."

"Oh," I said.

"I'm sorry, Mr. Zinsser."

"Me too, Kathy."

"You've got to understand that all media like this are subject to loss."

"I understand."

"O.K.," she said. "Well, goodbye. Have a nice day."

# 9. Some Precautions

My chat with Kathy left me shaken. The worst had happened. Now I wanted to think about keeping it from ever happening again.

But first I sat down at my old Underwood standard typewriter and tried to recover my document. If what I had written was out in the electricity, maybe some stray currents were still circulating in the room, or in my brain. Could I catch them before they evaporated, or went wherever electricity goes?

I began to type, and fragments of the morning's prose came limping back: phrases, clauses, half-sentences, whole sentences. They weren't in quite the right order, and some of them had gone so far into the electricity that they didn't come back at all. But at least my work wasn't totally lost.

My feelings about the process were mixed. Manually, the typewriter seemed stiff and heavy—it was a chore to pound the keys and to operate the carriage return. Emotionally, however, it was consoling to see my words emerge on paper. Good old paper. No amount of electricity was going to pluck those words off the paper and spirit them away. I began to unwind. My pulse returned to normal typing speed.

Still, it was hardly the ideal method of writing: compose, lose and conjure back. Obviously I ought to review what had gone wrong and see what lessons it would teach me.

I called Robert at IBM. I was feeling very resentful: what kind of turkey had he sold me? But Robert had been assigned to a new district. Could Harriet help me? She was the new marketing representative for my account.

I asked for Harriet and told her about IBM's faulty program diskette and about my wonderful prose being out in the electricity. She was sorry. She reminded me that it was important to keep transferring what I wrote to my work diskette, where it would be preserved. "Otherwise it exists only in the machine's memory," she said, "and it gets lost whenever you turn the power off."

I thanked her and she told me to have a nice day and I went back to my machine. But I was still puzzled. How could my words be lost if they were in the machine's memory? Surely "memory" is what is remembered. But it's not. I realized that this was another problem of terminology. Memory, in the world of word processors, is temporary. The word applies to what you have been typing until you transfer it to a diskette for storage. The machine holds your words in its "memory" while you are working on them so that you can keep looking at them and changing them.

You'll grasp this fact more easily if you visualize where the memory is. The memory is inside the electronic module that the screen sits on top of. It's part of the equipment that is actually enabling you to write; it's not off to one side, like the diskette unit, which is for storing what you have written, or like the printer, which is for printing what you have stored.

Another helpful fact to keep in mind is that the memory has a limit to what it will hold: approximately 1,000 words.

After that it will automatically start moving words over to the work diskette to be stored. This means that you can lose up to 1,000 words while typing if anything goes wrong with the equipment or the power.

Incidentally, the memory is sometimes called the "buffer." This strikes me as a much better term. Unlike memory, "buffer" implies an intermediate stage—which is exactly what it is. Your newly composed words are just visiting in limbo, and you leave them there at your own risk.

One obvious way to save what you have just written is to print it and get it on paper. But this is a separate process and therefore an inconvenience. You should save the printing of a chunk of writing until you have finished writing it.

The other way is to keep getting your words out of the machine's memory, which is fallible and fleeting, and onto a diskette.

But how can you remember to do this? You don't want to be nagged in the act of writing by the constant fear of loss. The easiest solution is to press the PAGE END key at the end of every "page" that you type. The average page holds sixty-one lines, and the machine will emit a *beep* at the end of every page. (If you want fewer lines per page you can default the disk accordingly.) When you hear the *beep*, press the PAGE END key. This removes the page you have just typed from the screen—and from the "memory"—and puts it on your work diskette. You'll hear a brief clunking in the diskette unit, presumably signifying that the transfer is taking place. The next thing you see will be a blank screen, or new "page," ready for you to continue writing.

If you secure every page when you get to the end, the only page you'll lose in a mishap is the one you're working on. That's a lot better than having 1,000 words vanish into the electricity.

# 10.   More Troubles

Harriet brought me a new program diskette and I was back in business. But not for long. My first breakdown was quickly followed by several others. Actually it was the equipment that was having breakdowns, not me. Or was it?

I had only been typing for about an hour with my new program diskette when I saw another 900 number on my screen. The sight was extraordinarily depressing. Again, everything stopped. Again, I called the Dallas hotline. This time I got a country and western song while waiting for a systems analyst. Stephanie was her name, and she listened patiently as I recited the thirty-seven digits of my latest hotline number.

When I got to the end she said that my software was O.K.; the failure was somewhere in the hardware. I should report it to IBM in New York, she said, and have them send over a customer engineer.

"You mean a repairman?" I asked. She said IBM called them customer engineers. High technology breeds noble language.

I thanked Stephanie and called my customer engineer. He said he would be over in the morning. That was on Monday afternoon. Meanwhile I was immobilized. I couldn't print or even summon back onto the screen what I had been working on.

On Tuesday morning the customer engineer came and diagnosed the problem: the memory was broken. He would get a new part and replace it that afternoon. Another day lost. I did some writing on my Underwood standard. By midafternoon I started to get edgy. Where was the customer engineer? (By now I was beginning to think of him as the repairman.) Why didn't he come? I put in another call. My desk was piling up with scraps of paper on which I had scribbled IBM telephone numbers and 900 numbers. The repairman said he couldn't get the part for one more day. He'd bring it on Wednesday.

On Wednesday two men came with their tools and operated on my machine. They took the top off, revealing its innards. I peered over their shoulders like an anxious parent. It wasn't that I wanted to know how the various circuits worked; I just thought I ought to be solicitous.

I suppose I also wanted to find out what was behind the all-knowing screen. For several weeks the machine had been telling me what to do, carrying out some of my wishes, balking at others, and chiding me for my stupidities. It was still the master and I the slave. In fact, I was struck by how often I found myself feeling badly for putting the machine to extra work or making it do a certain job again. It would clunk laboriously, bringing back to the screen some item I had sent away by mistake, and I would have a flash of guilt and catch myself apologizing. Only after the moment had passed did I realize that it was absurd to feel sorry for a bunch of lights and wires. But I couldn't help it. I was still what I had always been—science's timid soul.

Now, however, the repairman had pried off the sleek exterior panel of my machine, and I felt as if the curtain had been pulled away that concealed the Wizard of Oz. No wizard, only Professor Marvel; no omnipotent computer, only a lot of screws and circuits. At that point the machine lost some of its power over me. It's nothing but some kind of crazy typewriter, I thought. Of such small insights the beginning writer begins to accumulate his own small chips of wisdom.

The repairman took out the faulty memory—a piece of cardboard with a network of circuits on it—and slipped a new memory in. He closed everything up, like a good surgeon, and told me I could write again.

I said I didn't think it boded well that a brand new machine had broken so soon. I think my actual words were: "What the hell's the matter with this thing? Can't you guys get the damn bugs out of it or have I got some kind of crappy lemon?" The repairman looked at me with equanimity; I gathered that he had heard this phrasing of the question before. Still, I felt better being able to rail at an actual person. To swear at the machine, as I frequently did, was meager solace. To snap at Kathy was a better release, but Kathy was in far-off Dallas. What could she do? It fell on the repairman to repair not only my memory but my testy mood.

"We find that most of the breakdowns occur in the first month," he explained. "A number of little things can go wrong when these units are packed and shipped and installed in a new location." That made sense, though I was then almost beyond logic. I thanked the repairman for coming, squiring him to the door with the elaborate gratitude that we shower on doctors who have put us out of pain, and he left.

My travails, however, were not over. On Thursday still another code number on the screen told me that still another function was amiss. Again, all work came to a halt, and I summoned still another repairman. He checked the machine and announced that I had a software problem. He said it with a certain hauteur, which I translated to mean: "Don't look at me—the hardware's all right. Can I help it if you've got bum software that you're putting into my equipment?" It was my first glimpse of the fact that in the computer technician's world, hardware and software are two different breeds. It's like talking to a dog lover about cats, or, worse, to a cat lover about dogs. But to the immobilized writer it couldn't matter less whether the ware is hard or soft. All I knew was that my machine was busted.

The repairman said that my program diskette—the new one that the company had supplied only a few days before—had some imperfection and no longer worked. Maybe a scratch. Maybe a little dust. Maybe somebody put something heavy on top of it.

I said that I thought these diskettes were supposed to be permanent. Weren't we always being told to get our stuff out of the memory and onto the disk, where it was safe?

Look, he said, nothing is safe. "Some guy could come in here and spill coffee on your diskette and you'd lose your whole book."

"I'd *what?*" He had spoken the unspeakable. I babbled something. It was a good week for babbling.

"What you should always do," he said, "is make a duplicate. Whenever you get a new program diskette from the company, make a copy of it on a work diskette of your own and put it away someplace. Then if something happens to the program diskette you're not stuck; you can use your duplicate and keep going. Same thing with your work diskette. At the end of the day you should make a duplicate of what you've written."

It was another small chip in the beginning of wisdom. I saw that I would always be at the mercy of mechanical breakdown. Hardware and software would both fail me— probably at the worst time. But I also saw that I could take some precautions that would leave me less paralyzed—and would also reduce my house calls from customer engineers and my chats with systems analysts in Dallas. It wasn't that I didn't like talking to Kathy and Stephanie. But if I had my choice of subjects to talk to them about, it wouldn't be hardware and software.

# 11. Disks

My troubles went away as abruptly as they had come. My equipment calmed down, and so did I, and I began to do some writing every day. I never quite lost the feeling that the equipment was likely to fail at any moment, but as a succession of days passed and nothing went wrong I started to relax. My relationship with my machine improved. I turned to it routinely, as I had always turned to my typewriter, and certain processes even became automatic.

But I gave more thought to the care and protection of my disks. I saw that I had been treating them far too casually. All the talk of getting my words out of mere electricity and onto sturdy disks had lulled me into the notion that the disks were actually sturdy. Now they suddenly seemed quite fragile.

I also realized for the first time that disks are the heart of the system. Until then I had been comforted by the fact that I would always be able to print what I wrote and thereby get it preserved on paper. But that wasn't the point of the new technology. The point—especially for businesses and other offices—was to be able to store on disks a vast number of documents that could be used again and again, with slight additions or changes. The disk—not paper—is the word processor's filing system. Files in the office of tomorrow will consist mainly of disks, waiting to have their contents summoned onto a screen and consulted and used in some new way, or in the same old way, once more. Filing and duplicating and protecting disks will be the job of every officeperson, not just every secretary.

Here are some basic things to know about disks:

Disks, or diskettes, are about eight inches square and they look somewhat like the old 45 rpm phonograph records. They are commonly called "floppy disks" because they are not as stiff as phonograph records. But they aren't *really* floppy—like, say, jello. They are encased in a plastic jacket that should never be removed. The jacket has several small openings where the magnetic surface of the disk is exposed, and it is through these openings, presumably, that information is put onto the disk or taken off. Exactly how this happens I am not now nor will I ever be in a position to say. It is enough that the machine knows how to do it.

You should try not to touch the magnetic surface of the disk when you handle the plastic jacket; oily fingerprints are not the kind of input it wants. Don't let your disks get bent. Keep them away from smoke, from sunlight and from magnetic objects. Don't put heavy objects on them, like books or ashtrays. Don't attach anything to them with a paper clip or a rubber band. Don't write on the plastic jacket or the outer paper envelope with a pencil or a ballpoint pen, which could press through to the disk; use a felt pen for writing a label that identifies the disk's contents.

I feel like a heretic for giving such advice. Writers are a messy breed, and nothing so dries their creative juices as a desk that is neat and clean. Show me a writer's desk and I will show you a desk with some substance that's positively asking to be spilled onto what the writer is writing: food, candy, coffee, Coke, tobacco. These are the natural lubricants of his craft. Unfortunately, they are not the natural lubricants of electronic equipment. Little as I know about computer technology, I suspect that it wouldn't take more than a few crumbs of Danish pastry to knock your software out for the day.

Therefore you should develop good habits, however alien this idea may be. If you must spill, spill on yourself. You can get your pants back from the cleaner faster than you can get a new program diskette.

The program diskette is a patented program that belongs to the company that manufactures or markets your computer. You can't buy it in a retail outlet; you obtain it and pay for it with your initial purchase or lease. But once you have it you can duplicate it on a blank work diskette. Blank diskettes can be bought easily, and you should always keep a few on hand.

The procedure for duplicating a diskette is simple. This doesn't mean that I *thought* it would be simple. In fact, I assumed it would be so intricate that I kept postponing my first solo. Finally, as in so many other cases, I just decided to take a chance that if the machine said it could duplicate a diskette it probably could.

The first step is to get the TASK SELECTION MENU on your screen. Press the key to choose WORK DISKETTE TASKS. This will bring you the WORK DISKETTE MENU, which lists various tasks. Choose the task called DUPLICATE DISKETTE. This will give you a menu that asks you what diskette you want to make a copy of. Put that disk in the left slot of your diskette unit. (If it's the program diskette it will already be there.) Let's say that its name is IBMABC. Then put the blank diskette in the right slot, where it will be ready to receive the contents of the diskette in the left slot. The screen will ask you to give the new diskette a name. Let's say that your name is Jones and you name the blank diskette JONES. The screen will display the plan that you hope to execute. It will tell you what disk you are about to duplicate "from" (IBMABC) and what diskette the material is going "to" (JONES). Read it and make sure that this is what you really want to do. If it is, press ENTER.

No step can be executed on a word processor, incidentally, until you press ENTER. What the key means is "Do it." Even if you want to delete—a step for which the proper word would seem to be "exit"—the key to press is ENTER. I became very grateful for the pause for final consideration that the ENTER key provides. If you instruct the machine to do something and then change your mind, you're still safe; just press CANCEL (which means what it says) and your instructions will be cancelled. The machine won't do anything until it gets your actual command, which is ENTER.

When I pressed ENTER to duplicate a diskette for the first time, I didn't really think it would duplicate my diskette. This was typical of my attitude in the early weeks. The machine was just pretending that it could do all that stuff. In fact, whenever I tried any new step I always waited with childlike curiosity to see what the machine would actually do—as opposed to what I had asked it to do and what it said it would do. This introduced an element of suspense into my days that IBM could never have imagined in its weirdest fantasies.

In this case, however, I saw to my surprise—in the space above the green line—the words DUPLICATING DISKETTE. The machine was really duplicating my diskette! I heard clicking and clunking noises in the diskette unit that I took to be diskette-duplicating noises. Was I really to believe that all the chips of information on the "from" diskette were being copied on the "to" diskette? Through those little holes? It didn't seem the least bit likely.

But then the words above the green line changed to DISK-ETTE DUPLICATED. The deed was done—or so I was being told. Would the machine lie to me? Sure it would. What better revenge on a person who doesn't trust machinery? Just as a horse can tell when its rider is afraid, I was sure that my machine could feel, spreading through its ganglia from my fingertips on the keys, the chill of nonbelief.

There was only one way to find out. I took the formerly blank diskette out of the right slot and put it in the left slot and summoned its contents onto the screen. The contents were the same as the material on IBM's program diskette. I was genuinely surprised. But I was also elated. I had performed an important work diskette task. So had the machine. After that, duplicating a diskette would never be so traumatic again.

But the procedure does have one pitfall—in fact, a chasm—to trap the unwary. This is where you can suffer the ultimate disaster: erasing your entire disk by mistake. I will try to explain. Listen carefully.

When you copy Diskette A (left slot) onto Diskette B (right slot), everything on Diskette B is automatically erased before any copying occurs. In most cases this doesn't matter. If Diskette B is a blank disk, for instance, there is nothing on it to erase. Or suppose you are writing a book on Diskette A and have completed fifty pages. You have already made a duplicate of those fifty pages on Diskette B. (A wise precaution and good disk discipline.) Your next day of writing goes well and you write ten more pages—that's sixty altogether on Diskette A. But you only have fifty of those pages on Diskette B, and you want all sixty. So you decide to duplicate Diskette A on Diskette B. When I first did this I assumed that the machine would simply add the ten new pages to what was already there. But this is not how the machine works. It erases the existing fifty pages and replaces them with the full sixty pages.

I tell you this for two reasons. One is so that you won't jump out of your skin with panic when you first use the DUPLICATE menu and you read on the screen that the entire contents of the "TO" diskette will be erased. It's a terrible moment: everything you've written is about to vanish forever. Not until you press the CANCEL key to avert this calamity does your heartbeat slow down enough for you to read the manual and learn that what vanishes will be instantly replaced.

The other reason is so that you won't inadvertently erase some material that will *not* be replaced from Diskette A.

Assume, for example, that you have written a twenty-page article called SMITH on Diskette A. As a precaution you want to duplicate it on another diskette, and you choose Diskette C, on which you have already written a twenty-page article called "BROWN." You know that every diskette will hold at least one hundred pages, so there's obviously plenty of room, and you assume that the machine will just add the contents of Diskette A (SMITH) to some part of Diskette C that is not occupied by BROWN. It won't. As I explained above—were you really listening?—BROWN will go into the electricity. And you will go to the nearest bar.

If you are writing a document that grows from day to day—a book, say, or a long article—a good discipline is to duplicate your work diskette at the end of every day. In that way you will always have a copy of what you have written. If anything happens to the original diskette you haven't lost any material. You won't have to write it or type it again.

Obviously another way to preserve what you have written

is to print it at the end of every day. For a writer this is almost a biological need—to see the manuscript actually taking shape. It's not enough to know that the manuscript already exists on a diskette; paper is the physical proof of that shadowy fact.

At first it was important to me to print what I had written and to read it over. The rising pile of paper told me that I was indeed writing a book, and I could also show parts of it to other people. (Until then I think it was inconceivable to my friends at the office that I was performing a creative act. They saw me hunched at my terminal like a grim technician. Surely I was not *writing*.)

But surprisingly soon I lost my need for paper. I would write for as much as a week without printing what I had written. Whenever I started to write and wanted to review what had gone before, I called the pages onto the screen and reviewed them there. The green letters, arrayed in tidy paragraphs, no longer struck me as cold and futuristic. The sentences looked like my sentences, and I studied them as objectively as if they had been on paper, seeing, as always, much that I didn't like—unnecessary phrases and adjectives, inexact words, lapses of order and logic. But now I could make instant repairs with my wonderful new keyboard and all its wonderful new keys.

I was not only weaning myself away from paper. I was learning to trust the system and to think in terms of disks as a basic writer's tool.

# 12.  The Keyboard

We come now to the all-important keyboard. Everything else is secondary—the disks, the "memory," the printer. Like the strings and hammers of a piano, they exist only to execute what the person at the keyboard transmits from his mind to his fingers.

I felt comfortable at the keyboard of my word processor almost immediately because I've been typing all my life. On the whole I'm not manually adept—I can't sew on a button and I can hardly open a boiled egg. But I can do two things well that require more motor coordination than sewing on a button: I can type and I can play the piano. I can probably do these things because I want to do these things. I definitely want to play the piano more than I want to open boiled eggs.

What this means is that someone starting on a word processor without being able to type well—or at all—must want to be able to use the machine. Dexterity, I suspect, is ultimately in the head, not the hands. But you shouldn't be scared off. Learning to type isn't one of life's hardest tasks; millions of people have done it. I taught myself very early by the inelegant hunt-and-peck method and only later learned the touch system. To use the word processor I just had to

master a few new keys—mainly the four cursor keys, the
DELETE key, the BACKSPACE key and the ENTER key.

Here, briefly, is how they work.

The cursor is a line of light that moves across the screen as
you write. It is only as wide as one letter and it is always
directly under the space where you want to type next. If it
isn't, you can move it to where you *do* want to type next. It
is, in short, a pointer. You move the cursor around like a
pointer to tell the machine, "I want the next thing I type to
go right here."

Much of the time, of course, the cursor will be at rest
where you stopped typing a sentence, waiting for your next
sentence. When you start that sentence the cursor will start
moving again, staying one space to the right of every letter
that you type. You can use the space bar to move it another
space to the right, just as you use the space bar on a typewriter to move the carriage. If you want to start a new paragraph at the end of a sentence, push the RET (carriage return)
key and the cursor will move down to the next line.

Four different keys enable you to move the cursor in four
different directions: left, right, up, down. Each key has an
arrow to indicate which way it makes the cursor move.
When you press a key it moves the cursor one space. But if
you hold the key down it moves the cursor rapidly across the
screen, or up and down the screen.

If you want to move the cursor even faster—and you often
do—you can press a special key called CODE together with
the cursor key. This instructs the cursor to move instantly as
far as it can go in the direction of the arrow. At the end of a
line, for example, you may want to go back to the beginning
of the line to correct the first word. Press the CODE key and
the *left* arrow key; the cursor will be there faster than you
can see it go. Or if you're at the bottom of a page and you

want to see what's at the top of the page, press the CODE key and the *up* arrow: the screen will display the top portion of the page, and the cursor will be under the first letter of the first word.

The *up* and *down* cursor keys are what you use to bring more lines of what you have written into view. A page will accommodate sixty-one lines of typing, but the screen can only display twenty lines at a time. This means that if you want to see what you wrote in an earlier paragraph that's no longer on the screen, you have to "scroll" the page into view, using the *up* cursor key to bring the preceding lines down. (You use the *down* cursor to bring lower lines up.) How this affects the act of writing—not being able to look at more than a small chunk of your work—I'll consider in a later chapter. Now I just want to explain how the various keys work.

What makes the system so enjoyable is that anything you type at the location of the cursor will displace what is already there. It won't lose the existing sentences; it will just push them to the right. This means that wherever you place the cursor you can insert a new word, a new phrase, a new sentence, or any number of new paragraphs. Assume, for instance, that you want to insert a new sentence in this paragraph—after the sentence that begins: "It won't lose." Just move the cursor back until it's under the *T* in "This means . . ." As you type your new sentence, the existing sentence ("This means . . .") will move to the right, one space at a time, accommodating as much as you want to add. Then the expanded paragraph will regroup itself in tidy lines.

Often, of course, when you put something new into a paragraph you will also want to take something out. Much of the inserting that you do with the cursor, for instance, will consist of replacing one word with a better word. When you

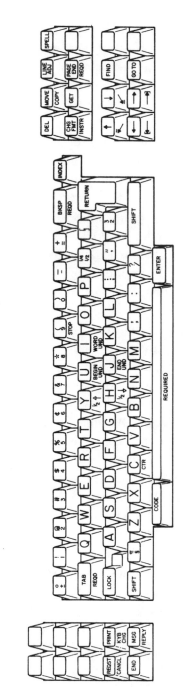

**THE KEYBOARD.** The keyboard of the IBM Displaywriter. Essentially it is similar to the keyboard of an electric typewriter, with the special keys for word processing functions grouped primarily in the extra sections at the left and at the right.

The special keys that you'll use most often are the four cursor keys, just to the right of the main keyboard, which have arrows denoting the direction in which they will move the cursor; the DEL (delete) key at the top of that section; the BKSP (backspace) key, which erases letters—and therefore erases common typing mistakes—as it moves backward over what you have just written; and the ENTER key, at the bottom of the main keyboard, which executes all your commands.

Functions that are shown on the front face of a key can be activated only by pressing the CODE key at the same time. The word CANCL, for instance, is on the front face of the REQST key at the left. If you change your mind about an instruction and want to CANCEL it, press the CODE key and the REQST key. The four cursor keys also have a special function that is indicated on their face. If you want to move the cursor instantly across the page to the right margin, or back to the left margin, or up to the top line of the page or down to the bottom line, press the CODE key and the appropriate cursor key.

type in the better word, the one that you are discarding will move along to the right. Then you have to delete it with the DELETE key. Thus the cursor and the DELETE key become the writer's twin companions as he ranges over the screen, rewriting and rearranging, cutting and condensing. I soon learned to use them with pleasure, for I'm well aware that very few sentences are born perfect. Almost every sentence has, among other failings, more words than it needs. To get rid of the extra words with the mere flick of an electronic wand is enormously satisfying.

Which brings us to the DELETE key.

When you want to delete anything from the screen, move the cursor to the letter where you want to start deleting. You may want to delete only one letter. Move the cursor under that letter and press DELETE. The letter will instantly be framed in a box of green light that is brighter than all the other letters. The green box encloses what you have told the machine you want to delete. Simultaneously the screen asks you: DELETE WHAT? If the box correctly expresses your wishes, press ENTER and the doomed letter will vanish.

But you will usually want to delete more than one letter— in fact, whole words, clauses, sentences. What then?

Again, move the cursor to the first letter in the sequence of words that you want to get rid of. Press DELETE. The screen will ask: DELETE WHAT? You will tell it what to delete.

How will you do this? Here's a passage from Thoreau's *Walden* that we can tinker with:

For my part, I could easily do without the post-office. I think there are very few important communications that are made through it. To speak critically, I never received more than one or two letters in my life—I wrote this some years ago—that were worth the postage. And I am sure that I never read any memorable news in a newspaper. If we read of one man robbed, or murdered, or killed by accident, or one house burned, or one vessel wrecked, or one steamboat blown up, or one cow run over on the Western Railroad, or one mad dog killed, or one lot of grasshoppers in the winter, we never need read of another. One is enough.

Assume that you want to delete the first three words. You can do it in various ways. First, move the cursor under the *F* and press the DELETE key. Only the *F* will be boxed in green light. Move the cursor another space to the right. The *o* will also be boxed in green. Keep moving the cursor to the right and each successive letter, plus the comma and the space, will be boxed in green. Press ENTER; the first three words and the comma and the space will disappear, and the remaining words ("I could easily . . .") will slide over to the left, replacing what has gone.

But this is a slow and bothersome method: you have to press the cursor key thirteen times to blanket all the characters you want to delete. Much swifter solutions are available. They operate on a simple principle: After the system asks "Delete what?" it will delete everything through and including whatever character you strike on the keyboard next.

For example (going back to Thoreau), if you start with the cursor under the first *F*, press DELETE and then press a comma, the machine will highlight in a green box all the characters it encounters until it finds the first comma—in this case, the comma after "part." Press ENTER and the first three words and the comma will go. But you'll still be left with a space that you don't want. The cursor will be poised at that space, having deleted all the preceding characters. Press

DELETE, press ENTER, and the space will go. That's a two-step delete, which is better than a thirteen-step delete.

But there's a still easier method—one that quickly became habitual for me. That method is to use the space bar as the instruction for deleting. Remember that the machine thinks of a space as just another character, like a letter of the alphabet. Therefore if the machine asks "Delete what?" and you press the space bar once, the machine will delete everything through and including the first space. For example (going back to Thoreau again), if you press the space bar three times, you will see highlighted in a green box the first three words ("For my part") plus the comma and the final space. Press ENTER and the deleting is instantly done.

The great advantage of the space-bar method is that much of your deleting will consist of just one word plus the space that follows it. This is true, for instance, when you substitute one word for another. Suppose you don't like the word "easily" in Thoreau's first sentence and want to replace it with "happily." Move the cursor under the *e* in "easily" and type the new word in. "Easily" will make room for it by moving along to the right, but you still have to get rid of it. Move the cursor under the *e* in "easily," press DELETE, press the space bar, and press ENTER. "Easily" will go and your spacing will be correct.

You'll also find a lot of brief phrases—three or four words long—that are ripe for deleting. They are clutter phrases, separated from the rest of the sentence by commas, which don't do any real work: "on the whole," "I might add," "in a very real sense." Now you can kill them off with one quick tap of the DELETE key and three or four quick taps of the space bar. Consider, as an exercise, how you might thin out the nine forms of "news" cited by Thoreau in the sentence beginning "If we read." You could prune the list very rapidly if you wanted to. (I wouldn't want to; Thoreau usually knew what he was doing.)

You'll soon get these various patterns in your eye and learn to make the combination of moves that will do your deleting with the greatest speed and economy.

Suppose, for example, you want to delete Thoreau's entire first sentence. Put the cursor under the first *F*, press DELETE, and then press a period. Press ENTER and the machine will delete everything through the period after "post-office." Or suppose you want to delete Thoreau's first two sentences. Press the period twice. The machine will highlight everything through the first period (after "post-office") and will proceed until it meets a second period (after "it"). Everything in the first two sentences will be instantly highlighted. Look at it and make sure it's what you want to delete. If it is, press ENTER and the first two sentences will go.

The trick is to look ahead in your copy to find some distinctive letter or character that the machine will race ahead to reach. It might be a quotation mark closing a quotation. Your eye tells you that you want to delete the entire quotation, which might consist of many sentences. If you press a period you will delete only the first sentence; if you press a quotation mark you'll delete the entire quotation.

The dash is another punctuation mark that serves this function. For example: if you want to delete the parenthetical phrase in the middle of Thoreau's third sentence—"I wrote this some years ago"—just put the cursor under the first dash and instruct the machine to delete everything through the second dash.

Still another key that you can use as a final marker is the RET (carriage return) key. To the machine this key denotes the end of a paragraph. Therefore if you want to delete an entire paragraph, just press the RET key, and all the sentences in the paragraph will be framed in light green. Press ENTER and they will vanish.

This is always a heady moment—the moment when you can make so much writing just disappear. But it's also somewhat scary. Fortunately, you always have a chance to review your decision before you press the fateful ENTER. If you see that you highlighted more words than you want to delete, don't panic. Just press CANCEL and start over.

There's one other method of deleting, which works on a different principle. But it's the method that you'll use more than any other. This is because it's not for making decisions about the writing, but for erasing common typing mistakes. Even the best typists make a lot of mistakes. The machine knows this and has given you the BACKSPACE key to wipe your sins away. This is one area, at least, where it has no Calvinist hang-ups about human fallibility.

The BACKSPACE key simply erases every character that it meets as it moves backward through what you have just written. It erases one letter at a time with each press of the key; if you hold the key down it moves faster. This makes the key ideal for instantly correcting wrong letters and leaving no mess. There's no xxx'ing, no erasing, no white-out.

Assume that you hit an extra key in this sentdence. Just backspace over it: the period and the last five letters will vanish, and then you'll type the last four letters and the period again. The whole job takes five seconds—and takes less thought and fewer different moves than the DELETE key.

All these decisions soon become instinctive. You begin to know at a glance which keys will do the fastest job of deleting the words and letters you want to get rid of.

The keys that I've just described are the ones you'll use constantly: the four cursor keys, DELETE, ENTER and BACK-

SPACE. I'll mention several others and end this brief tour of the keyboard.

GO TO is a key that tells the machine to go to a certain page. You know you stopped typing yesterday in the middle of page 22, and that's where you want to resume today. You could get there by starting on page 1 and pressing the *down* cursor key; eventually you would reach page 22. Instead, press GO TO. The machine will ask you to type the number of the page where you want to go. Type "22," press ENTER and you'll instantly see the cursor poised at the top of that page.

FIND is a key that reaches the same goal by a different route. You don't remember the page where you stopped writing. But you do remember that you were working on a passage where you used a proper name or an unusual word that you hadn't used up to that point. Let's say the name was Xerxes. (This is the passage with your brilliant allusion to the Persian Wars.) Press FIND. The machine will ask: Find what? Type "Xerxes" and press ENTER. The machine will clunk self-importantly for a few seconds and the page that you're looking for will appear on the screen, with the cursor under the *X*. If you're looking for that charming reference to ptarmigan . . . but you get the point. The machine will move through a body of writing until it finds a combination of letters that hasn't previously appeared.

MOVE is a key that you will put to many uses. It will move any chunk of writing from one place to another. You can move sentences around within a paragraph, for instance, or to another paragraph. You can move whole paragraphs. You can move material from one page to another, or even from one diskette to another. When you press the MOVE key, the screen will ask MOVE WHAT? You indicate with the cursor the material that you want to move. Then the screen will ask MOVE WHERE? You take the cursor to the place where you want the material to go. Then you press ENTER and pray. Remarkably, the material gets moved.

END is the key that you press when you finish writing—and before you take the diskette out. When you press END everything that you have just written will be transferred to your work diskette and added to what you have already stored there. If you take your diskette out before you press END you will lose what you have just written. This will also happen—you will lose what you have just written—if you turn the power switch off before you press END.

Obviously it's very important to press END whenever you're going to stop writing. Make this not only a discipline; make it a reflex. After you press END, the next thing you'll see on the screen will be a menu with a list of tasks to choose from. Whenever you see a menu, you can safely take your diskettes out. Then you can turn off the power.

Then you're on your own power.

# 13.   Pagination

Pagination! I have always loved the word and been sorry that it doesn't mean all the things I think it ought to mean. Its sound wafts me to romantic or faraway worlds. I think of the great voyages that paginated the Indies. I watch the moon-light playing across the pagination on the Taj Mahal. I hear glorious music (Lully's pagination for trumpets). I savor gourmet meals (mussels paginated with sage). I see beautiful women—the pagination on their bodice catches my eye—and dream of the nights we will spend in torrid pagination. The wine that we sip will be exquisitely paginated—dry, but not too dry—and as the magical hours slip away we will . . .

But why torture myself? The fact is that it's a dumb word that means just one thing: the process of arranging pages in their proper sequence and getting them properly numbered. It's something we all do, every day, almost without thought. We paginate every time we scribble a shopping list on a few scraps of paper. So much for the romance of pagination.

When you write on a word processor, of course, you don't have any paper to shuffle. But you still need to keep your pages in some kind of order. (Some kind of order is what you kept them in when you used to spread them out on the floor.) Therefore the machine has to do the job for you.

You don't have to keep telling the machine to paginate. It will paginate routinely, knowing that if it didn't you would go crazy. But frequently you will also need to get into the act. This happens, for instance, when you insert new material in an article that has already been paginated. The revised article will have to be paginated again to incorporate what you added. The machine won't do this, however, until you give it the word.

Essentially the system is simple. The screen always tells you—at the top—what page you are on and also what line the cursor is on. If you are starting to write an article, it will say page 1 at the top. When you get to the bottom of the page the line number will say 61. Remember that if you have programmed your machine to type your copy double-spaced, you will have only thirty lines of actual writing on a sixty-one-line page. On line 61 the machine will beep. Press the PAGE END key; you will be given a blank screen and at the top it will say page 2.

Of course, you don't have to fill the entire page with writing. If you finish a chapter halfway down page 5—on line 30—and you want to start the next chapter at the top of page 6, just keep pressing the RET (carriage return) key until the cursor gets down to line 61. Then press PAGE END; you'll get a new page that says page 6.

Remember, however, that there will always be thirty-one lines of blank space between the two chapters—you have just put them there. Later, when your document is revised and repaginated, the chapter endings may fall differently and you may not want that much space. In which case, you can use the DELETE key to remove as many of the blank lines as you want to get rid of. You do this by moving the cursor under the symbol for "carriage return" (it looks like an ar-

row) and then pressing DELETE. Just as you previously inserted blank lines by pressing the RET key, one line at a time, you
now reverse that process by deleting the RET symbol, one line
at a time.

This is a hard concept to grasp at first because you are
eliminating something that you can't see: blank lines. But the
larger principle is important for understanding the logic of
the whole system. You use the DELETE key not just to eliminate visible letters; you also use it to delete specifications that
you have programmed into your manuscript and that you no
longer want—in this case, empty space. In short, you delete
instructions in the same way that you delete words.

I bring up this point about the logic of the system to urge
you to trust your own powers of logic. Try to figure out how
the machine arrives at its requests and decisions. Soon you
will find yourself deducing—without having to rummage
around in the instruction book—how the machine probably
executes a certain task that you want it to do.

When I first did this I was elated. Until then I had assumed that I couldn't take any new step without getting specific directions from the manual. But as I became more re-
laxed I developed a sense of how the machine had been
programmed to "reason." I would think: "I want to do X.
My guess is that the machine would accomplish this by re-
quiring me to do Y and Z." Then I'd press the appropriate
keys and X would get accomplished.

I don't cite this as a feat of genius; even with a hangover I
should be able to outthink a bunch of wires that can only
make a yes-or-no choice. Still, up to that point the bunch of
wires had in fact seemed to be smarter. Mine was a small
victory for confidence—without which, as so many coaches
have reminded us, no game can be won. One of the great
first lines in any book is the opening sentence of Dr. Benja-
min Spock's *Baby and Child Care*: "You know more than

you think you do." More than thirty million mothers and fathers have been empowered by that sentence to do complex tasks that they never did before. My analogy isn't exact because babies are part of nature and word processors are not; we are more likely to know how to change a diaper than to initialize a diskette. Nevertheless I often thought of Spock's dictum and found it helpful.

What pagination ultimately does is to take your completed manuscript, with all its changes, and arrange it in final form, ready to be printed. It does not put page numbers on the pages that you will eventually print. The process that I'm describing is solely for your information as you write and edit; it's a numbering system that tells you where you are. To print numbers on your actual pages at the top or at the bottom—"headers" and "footers," as the system calls them—you must use another menu, the "Format Selection" menu, which requires you to use the INSTRUCTION key to indicate exactly where you want the headers or the footers to go. It's a separate procedure with various complicated options, so I'll let your own manual explain it to you—partly because my manual never did manage to explain it to me.

Back to pagination. Unless you are a very unusual writer you won't write any document perfectly the first time. You will go back over it at least once, and probably more often, adding new sentences and cutting old ones, stitching your story together. Frequently you will insert whole new paragraphs to make new points—points that you meant to make but didn't, points that amplify an idea you now think you ought to develop, points that use new facts you didn't know before. All this is basic to the act of writing, and if you were doing it on paper you would assemble all the marked-up pages in their proper order and then type the whole manuscript over neatly.

To get this done on a word processor you use the pagination menu, giving the machine your instructions. Until you do, the machine will stay with its original pagination.

Assume, for instance, that you write a first draft that runs to twenty-five pages. The machine will paginate it as you write, from 1 to 25. Then you go back and insert two new paragraphs on page 5. You might think that the machine would simply push the existing material along, changing the pagination as it goes, the final page now becoming page 26. It won't. The original page 6 will remain page 6, and the overflow material from page 5 will go on page 5.1. If there is more overflow it will go on pages 5.2, 5.3, 5.4, etc.

Similarly, if you cut various sentences and paragraphs as you revise your manuscript, the machine won't bring the subsequent material forward. You will be left with the gaps. In other words, when you finish revising your document the screen will represent what you have done. You'll see what you added—on pages that have spilled over—and you'll see where you removed material, on pages that have an empty patch.

Now use the pagination menu to consolidate both the gains and the losses into an orderly whole. Just summon the menu onto the screen, review the choices it offers, and press ENTER.

It will ask you, for instance, if you want to have your document paginated "on an exact line count." If you say yes, the machine will put exactly sixty lines on every page (thirty lines of actual typing if your material is double-spaced). But this method will often give you a "widow" at the top of the next page—a short line that has only one word, or two or three words. Widows don't look good, and most people try to avoid them. If you don't like widows, say no, and the machine will paginate on an "inexact line count." This is how it avoids widows. When it sees one coming along, it ends the page on line 61, keeping the widow at the bottom of the page, or on line 59, pushing the widow over to the second line of the next page.

But you don't have to reinstruct the machine every time you paginate. You can program it to paginate on an inexact line count every time. Then you just press ENTER and sit back and listen to the machine cleaning up your mess. First you'll see the words PAGINATING DOCUMENT at the top of the screen. This is the machine telling you what it has started to do. Then you'll hear a series of irregular clunking noises from the diskette unit. This is the machine working its way through your document, bringing lines forward or back, incorporating the fragmentary pages and closing up the gaps.

The noise may continue for five or ten minutes, depending on how long the document is. It's a metallic noise, not exactly pleasant, and yet it has a certain music, for it is the sound of the machine laboring to put your house in order. Sometimes there is a pause: the machine wonders how to negotiate a tricky crossing. Sometimes the clunks come in triumphant bunches: the machine has made it to the other side, brilliantly leaping across the ice floes.

Finally the clunks stop altogether and a message on the screen tells you that your document has been paginated. You are now ready to print it—almost. But first you should read it one more time, "scrolling" the pages from beginning to end, to see if the pagination has left any bad breaks. It probably has. You might find, for instance, that the last line on a page says CHAPTER III. The machine doesn't know that this is a lousy place for CHAPTER III to be; it was only asked to paginate, not to make aesthetic judgments. You therefore move CHAPTER III to the next page yourself, perhaps lowering it somewhat because you like your new chapter headings to have some air.

This, of course, ruins the rest of the pagination. So you

paginate it again, from that point on. The menu will ask you
where you want to begin paginating. Tell it the page number, press ENTER, and listen to the clunking again. In fact,
you may have to repeat the process several times.

Don't feel guilty—as I did at first—about putting your
equipment to so much extra work. It's the only way you'll
get all the kinks out of your finished manuscript. Besides, the
machine obviously loves to paginate. You're doing it a favor.

# 14.  Printing

The printer is the only other major element that you need to know about. It prints onto paper the words you have written at your keyboard, thereby giving them reality. Until that moment you have only seen your words on the screen, where they are as insubstantial as light. They are also preserved on a disk—or so you have been told. But surely they don't exist there as words; they are just bits of electronic information. Nobody ever curled up at night with a good disk. What comforts the writer initially is the knowledge that a printer is ready and waiting to turn the new technology back into the old.

Nevertheless I didn't develop any fondness for my printer. It weighed on me. It was too big and ponderous—still another contraption to master, another series of steps to execute and worry about. I wanted to be able to just push a button on my diskette unit and get a printout of what I had written. Instead I had to tend a separate machine, feeding it paper and listening for the imperious beeps that told me what it wanted to be fed.

The printer is the biggest of all the units: it's two feet wide and almost as deep. I installed mine on a table against the far wall of my office to get it out of sight and out of mind. If I had put all five of my units on the same table I would have felt dwarfed and paralyzed. I had to keep the process of printing removed from the process of writing.

Despite its size and august appearance, the printer is nothing more than an automatic typewriter. It has no life of its own. It is activated by the parent unit, to which it is connected by an umbilical cord that looks exactly like an electrical cable, and it will print only what is stored there. You have to tell the parent unit what you want the printer to print, and your instructions will be passed along.

The system gives you two procedures for getting your pages printed, depending on how you like to work.

The first and simplest method is to print each page immediately after you write it. Assume that you have just written page 1. Press the PRINT key; the screen will beep and write you a message telling you to switch the printer to ON. You get up and turn it on. The screen then gives you another beep and another message, this one telling you to load the printer with paper of a certain size. You put a piece of paper in the printer. Then you get another beep and a message telling you to START the printer. You do, and it prints page 1. Meanwhile the screen has moved you along to page 2, where you can resume your writing while page 1 is being printed.

But this is hardly a restful way to write. You have to keep jumping up and down and listening for beeps and pushing buttons. The method is mainly useful if you're just writing one page—say, a one-page memo—and want to get a copy of it immediately.

The second method enables you to print everything that you've written after you have finished writing it. Assume that you are writing a book. In the morning you start on page 51 and at the end of the day you're on page 63. (It's mostly dialogue and goes very fast.) You want to print the day's work, so you summon the PRINT menu onto the screen. It will ask you what page you want to print FROM. You write "51." Then it will ask you what page you want to print THROUGH. You write "63." Then you press ENTER and, obedient to the successive beeps, you turn the printer on, load the paper and start the printer printing. When it reaches the bottom of page 51 it will notify you with a beep. Take the page out, put in a new page, press START, and it will print page 52. Etc. Each page takes about three minutes to print, so it's roughly a forty-minute job.

This method, however, doesn't allow you to do any more writing on your "document" while part of it is being printed. You have to find other jobs to pass the time: editing copy, writing letters, reading, paying bills. Every time you hear a beep you stop editing copy and go and take a sheet of paper out of the machine and put another one in. It gets to be a drag. Still, there's satisfaction in the sound of the typewriter doing your final typing, and the manuscript that keeps emerging is so pristine that you hardly recognize it as something you wrote.

Greater speed can be easily bought. The printer that I've been describing is the slowest model. Its typing element is a metal ball of the kind used on electric typewriters, and although it seems to be going very fast it is only typing fifteen and one-half characters per second. The more expensive models operate with what is called a printwheel element and can type forty or sixty characters per second. I didn't think I needed such incredible speed.

I also didn't think I needed an automatic paper handler. This is a device—available as an extra option—that keeps feeding paper into the typewriter from a roll, and it eliminates the bother of getting up every three minutes. I didn't

order it because it looked intricate and I wanted to start as
simply as possible. But now that I've gratified my yen for
simplicity I have a yen for an automatic paper feeder. In
fact, it strikes me as a supreme luxury. What I'd like to do is
finish my writing for the day, get a beer, start the printer
and hear just one more beep after that—the one that tells me
that the entire job is done.

When I first had my word processor I was so spooked by
the printer that I didn't use it, or even go near it, for several
weeks. This was my anti-gadget phobia at work: the voice
inside me that always says, "If it looks complicated don't try
it." I was having enough anxiety just figuring out how the
keyboard and the screen and the disks worked. Why try to
tame the monster in the corner along with all the other mon-
sters?

The day came, of course, when I had to print something,
and I approached the printer with the nervous respect that
might be given to a cyclotron. Just pushing the ON switch—
and hearing the machine go on—gave me a sense of achieve-
ment. As I proceeded I kept hearing beeps from the parent
unit, meaning that it had a message for me, and by rushing
back to the screen and reading the message and then rushing
back to the printer and doing what the message said, I got
the printer to print my first page. And my second page. And
my third page. But the process took concerted effort, and
after that when I wanted to print something I had to crank
up my resolve to go through the whole laborious chore again.
Only after several weeks did I realize that the printer could
be operated by a not very bright child of five, and I began to
use it almost absentmindedly, not paying any more attention
to the beeps because I knew what the messages would say.

The printer, as I said, has no life of its own. It prints every
page exactly as that page appears on the terminal screen,

word for word, line for line, space for space. You can't make any adjustments on the printer itself except to change the typeface by putting in a different typing element. Otherwise, any special arrangement of words or margins or spacing that you want to see on the page must be programmed by you at the keyboard. You do this by using the various menus on the program diskette that govern margins, tabs, page numbers, line spacing and other such details. This is why I found printing such a grim obstacle at first. It's not that the printer itself is complex; it's that you have to decide from the various menus on the screen how to tell the printer what to do.

Even then the printer often refuses to do it. A petulant beep summons you to the screen for a message that says, for instance, DISKETTE ERROR; PRINT JOB CANCELLED. It does no good to protest, or to threaten, or even to cry. The print job has been cancelled and you won't get another word printed until you figure out what the ominous message means and what to do about it.

The most frequent cause of having your print job cancelled is that you wrote too many lines on a page. The printer is under orders not to print more than a certain number of lines—usually sixty-one. Knowing this, whenever you write you dutifully press the PAGE END key at line 61, or even at line 59. But often the printer balks anyway. LONG PAGE; PRINT JOB CANCELLED, it says, with obvious relish, and everything comes to a halt. You call the errant page back to the screen—a procedure that takes an annoying amount of time and thought—and move the extra line or two over to the next page. But that in turn may make the next page too long, and you don't want to keep pushing lines around forever. What you really want to be doing is printing. That's what you had started to do before you were so rudely stopped.

The best remedy is to paginate your document, beginning with the troublesome page that was too long and that you have now repaired. Another solution is to make a habit of paginating everything you write—however brief—before you print it. When the system does its own paginating it doesn't exceed the limit that the printer will accept. Why the system and I differ on the exact location of line 61 is one of those mysteries that the owner of a word processor learns not to even try to solve.

I'd like to be liberated from the printer, or at least from fretting about it. Luckily, that day is surely near. Just as our cities and towns now have copying centers that will duplicate what we have typed, I envision commercial shops that will print what we have written on a word processor. We will just bring them our disk—or send them our disk over the telephone. In its present form the printer is simply too big for most of us to install at home, along with the other four units. Something else would have to go: a child or a cat or a dog.

People who write on a word processor at their office won't regard printing as such a psychological burden. Unlike the individual owner, they will share a central printer with many other people writing at many other terminals. That printer will have an automatic paper feeder and an endless roll of paper and an endless supply of people willing to fiddle with it when it stops—anything to keep from writing. Printing will become just another routine office task, as easy as working the coffee machine and almost as important.

# 15.  Progress Report

It is now August. I've been writing this book for about six months, mostly after hours, and today I have reached page 100. The sight of that "100" at the top of the screen is remarkably satisfying. It means that I've written 25,000 words on my word processor, not counting all the thousands that I've deleted and sent into the electricity, so my machine and I must be getting along all right.

I hardly notice the five domineering units when I come to work now, and I no longer feel self-conscious as I sit at my keyboard and peer into my terminal. I'm convinced that this is how much of America's daily writing will be done in another five years. If I'm an oddity in our office today, I'll be part of the landscape tomorrow.

People still stand near the door and watch me as I write, but now they are hesitant to say anything. No such codes inhibit them when I am typing at my old typewriter. A person at a typewriter is just typing and may be interrupted without a twinge of guilt. But I am doing technology! I am a priest at the altar of a new religion. Visitors knock softly and tiptoe into the chancel.

"It's only a typewriter," I say, trying to put them at ease,

but they don't really believe it. And why should they? The
green letters on my screen don't look like typewriting; the
keyboard has many peculiar keys; the diskette unit is a sinis-
ter box. Who could feel at ease with these appliances? Not
my visitors.

I've had no further breakdowns—mechanical or emotional—since the flurry of mishaps in my first month. How long
ago that now seems. I wonder how Kathy is getting along,
out at the hotline center in Dallas. Those Texas summers can
get pretty rough. I really should give her a call. And Barbara. How can I forget the morning she came over and defaulted my program disk? Now I can default my own program
disk. At least I think I can. At least when I summon up the
program disk menu I don't break into a cold sweat; I only do
warm sweats. My heart doesn't fibrillate when the screen
writes me a warning message; it only skips a beat.

My eyes are also doing fine. Whenever I start to write I
still turn off my desk light and pull down the Venetian
blinds to eliminate the glare on the screen. (Anyone who can
operate a Venetian blind can operate a word processor.) But
I leave my ceiling lights on, so the room isn't dark; it's only
muted. If I ever forget to shut out the light from the window
my eyes get tired immediately. I also notice some eye fatigue
when I've been writing for two or three hours straight. But
on the whole this hasn't been the problem I expected it to be.

I haven't learned to do anything on the word processor
that I didn't need to do. Sometimes I dip into one of the
three enormous IBM instruction manuals to seek help on
some point I'm not sure of, and that feeling in my stomach
that I associate with my early days at the machine—call it
nausea—washes over me. If any single force is destined to
impede man's mastery of the computer, it will be the manual that tries to teach him how to master it. What overpow-
ering drowsiness awaits the pupil who enters that gray realm

of language. I'm always grateful if I can find what I need quickly and get out alive. It only takes one sentence to wipe out most of the confidence I've won. Almost any sentence will do: "Turn now to 'Creating the Reference Copy of the Repetitive Paragraphs' in the Work Samples section of the Work Station Procedures Guide to read the specific steps you should follow to create a Master Reference Copy." The chances of my turning to that section are about as good as my chances of becoming president of IBM. I shield my eyes and run for the door.

I've been printing this book as I go along. When I finish writing and editing and rewriting a chapter, I paginate it and get the printer to type it. I now have ninety-nine pages of my final manuscript, neatly typed, plus several Xerox copies. I could have instructed the printer to print extra copies of every page, but that seemed more burdensome than just having Xeroxes made of the original.

Friends who have seen my manuscript are all pleasantly surprised. It didn't occur to them that what I've been writing could be made accessible to them in a form they could read. Nobody was more relieved than my publisher. He assumed that he would have to sit at a terminal to read my manuscript—or, worse, that he would never be able to read it at all.

People are also surprised that the manuscript looks so good. They expected it to be typed in one of those ugly and barely legible typefaces that most computers spew out. But there's no need for computer blight. If you have a decent printer you can choose an element that has a decent typeface, just as you would on an electric typewriter. Many word processors don't yet have this capability; they're small or cheap models, designed primarily for numbers and not for words. But it's false economy to use such a model if you want what you write on a word processor to make a good

impression—on editors, for instance, or customers. My printer may be a boring companion, but it does nice typing.

What I finally intend to give my publisher, however, is not
my manuscript but my disk. The disk can then be converted
directly to phototype; I've already done the "typesetting,"
here at my own keyboard. Actually the book won't quite fit
on one disk—I just checked to see how much room is left.
You can do this at any time by asking the machine to display
on the screen an index of your disk's contents. It will list
every "document" that you've created and will tell you how
much of the disk has been used. I'm now on page 103 and
my status, the index says, is: AVAILABLE 6%; UNUSABLE 1%. It
doesn't say who is using the other 1%—there's nobody else
here at the keyboard. In any case, I'm nearing the end of the
trail with Disk 1. But the real marvel to me is that one small
disk will hold more than 25,000 words.

I still have no idea how my IBM system compares with the
word processors that are now being made by many other
companies. Brand names and product appraisals are no part
of this book; there will be no chapter called "Choosing the
Right Word Processor for You." I assume that I would have
had comparable experiences—both good and bad—if I had
done my shopping elsewhere. Nothing that I've written is
meant to imply an endorsement of IBM's system. My relationship has continued to be strictly that of an individual
customer. Any services that I've been given—the hotline, the
visits from systems engineers and repairmen—are part of the
standard customer contract.

I use my word processor far more routinely now—and not
just for writing this book. At the Book-of-the-Month Club I
do a lot of editing which, like all editing, involves a lot of
revising and rewriting and patching. Ordinarily I would do
much of it at my typewriter, as I always have—typing a

paragraph, taking the page out of the typewriter and crumpling it and throwing it away, typing another page, working on that page with a pencil, and then retyping what I had worked on, until at last everything was the way I wanted it. Now when I embark on these tasks I find myself turning on my word processor and inserting the disk that I have named BOMC. The revisions go much faster and at the end the printer prints me a clean copy.

I've heard that one of the traumas for writers at a word processor is that they can no longer rip a page out of their typewriter and crumple it in a fit of frustration and rage. They can't stand to give up this classic writer's release. I have no such withdrawal pains: I have gone electronic with my releases. Yesterday's crumpling of paper is today's double jab at the DELETE and ENTER keys and the instant vaporizing of sentences that refused to be gracefully born.

Recently I put this book aside for a few weeks to write a promised magazine article. The deadline was not far off and the piece loomed with unusual complexity, almost daring me to solve its many problems. I knew that it would take a great deal of rewriting. Nevertheless I attacked it boldly. I pulled my chair over to my Underwood typewriter, put in a sheet of paper and started to type. The touch was heavy; the writing limped; the keys struck sluggishly at the paper. My old friend seemed infinitely old.

I pulled the sheet of paper out and crumpled it and threw it away. Something made me not want to put another sheet of paper in the typewriter. I pulled my chair over to my word processor, turned it on, put in a fresh diskette, named it with my own name, named the document for the subject of the article, and started to write. It seemed like the most natural thing in the world.

# 16. The Act of Writing: One Man's Method

Writing is a deeply personal process, full of mystery and surprise. No two people go about it in exactly the same way. We all have little devices to get us started, or to keep us going, or to remind us of what we think we want to say, and what works for one person may not work for anyone else. The main thing is to get something written—to get the words out of our heads. There is no "right" method. Any method that will do the job is the right method for you.

It helps to remember that writing is hard. Most non-writers don't know this; they think that writing is a natural function, like breathing, that ought to come easy, and they're puzzled when it doesn't. If you find that writing is hard, it's because it *is* hard. It's one of the hardest things that people do. Among other reasons, it's hard because it requires thinking. You won't write clearly unless you keep forcing yourself to think clearly. There's no escaping the question that has to be constantly asked: What do I want to say next?

So painful is this task that writers go to remarkable lengths to postpone their daily labor. They sharpen their pencils and change their typewriter ribbon and go out to the store to buy more paper. Now these sacred rituals, as IBM would say, have been obsoleted.

When I began writing this book on my word processor I didn't have any idea what would happen. Would I be able to write anything at all? Would it be any good? I was bringing to the machine what I assumed were wholly different ways of thinking about writing. The units massed in front of me looked cold and sterile. Their steady hum reminded me that they were waiting. They seemed to be waiting for information, not for writing. Maybe what I wrote would also be cold and sterile.

I was particularly worried about the absence of paper. I knew that I would only be able to see as many lines as the screen would hold—twenty lines. How could I review what I had already written? How could I get a sense of continuity and flow? With paper it was always possible to flick through the preceding pages to see where I was coming from—and where I ought to be going. Without paper I would have no such periodic fix. Would this be a major hardship?

The only way to find out was to find out. I took a last look at my unsharpened pencils and went to work.

My particular hang-up as a writer is that I have to get every paragraph as nearly right as possible before I go on to the next paragraph. I'm somewhat like a bricklayer: I build very slowly, not adding a new row until I feel that the foundation is solid enough to hold up the house. I'm the exact opposite of the writer who dashes off his entire first draft, not caring how sloppy it looks or how badly it's written. His only objective at this early stage is to let his creative motor run the full course at full speed; repairs can always be made later. I envy this writer and would like to have his metabolism. But I'm stuck with the one I've got.

I also care how my writing looks while I'm writing it. The visual arrangement is important to me: the shape of the words, of the sentences, of the paragraphs, of the page. I don't like sentences that are dense with long words, or paragraphs that never end. As I write I want to see the design that my piece will have when the reader sees it in type, and I want that design to have a rhythm and a pace that will invite the reader to keep reading. O.K., so I'm a nut. But I'm not alone; the visual component is important to a large number of people who write.

One hang-up we visual people share is that our copy must be neat. My lifelong writing method, for instance, has gone like this. I put a piece of paper in the typewriter and write the first paragraph. Then I take the paper out and edit what I've written. I mark it up horribly, crossing words out and scribbling new ones in the space between the lines. By this time the paragraph has lost its nature and shape for me as a piece of writing. It's a mishmash of typing and handwriting and arrows and balloons and other directional symbols. So I type a clean copy, incorporating the changes, and then I take that piece of paper out of the typewriter and edit it. It's better, but not much better. I go over it with my pencil again, making more changes, which again make it too messy for me to read critically, so I go back to the typewriter for round three. And round four. Not until I'm reasonably satisfied do I proceed to the next paragraph.

This can get pretty tedious, and I have often thought that there must be a better way. Now there is. The word processor is God's gift, or at least science's gift, to the tinkerers and the refiners and the neatness freaks. For me it was obviously the perfect new toy. I began playing on page 1—editing, cutting and revising—and have been on a rewriting high ever since. The burden of the years has been lifted.

Mostly I've been cutting. I would guess that I've cut at least as many words out of this book as the number that remain. Probably half of those words were eliminated because I saw that they were unnecessary—the sentence worked fine without them. This is where the word processor can improve your writing to an extent that you will hardly believe. Learn to recognize what is clutter and to use the DELETE key to prune it out.

How will you know clutter when you see it? Here's a device I used when I was teaching writing at Yale that my students found helpful; it may be a help here. I would put brackets around every component in a student's paper that I didn't think was doing some kind of work. Often it was only one word—for example, the useless preposition that gets appended to so many verbs (order up, free up), or the adverb whose meaning is already in the verb (blare loudly, clench tightly), or the adjective that tells us what we already know (smooth marble, green grass). The brackets might surround the little qualifiers that dilute a writer's authority (a bit, sort of, in a sense), or the countless phrases in which the writer explains what he is about to explain (it might be pointed out, I'm tempted to say). Often my brackets would surround an entire sentence—the sentence that essentially repeats what the previous sentence has said, or tells the reader something that is implicit, or adds a detail that is irrelevant. Most people's writing is littered with phrases that do no new work whatever. Most first drafts, in fact, can be cut by fifty percent without losing anything organic. (Try it; it's a good exercise.)

By bracketing these extra words, instead of crossing them out, I was saying to the student: "I may be wrong, but I think this can go and the meaning of the sentence won't be affected in any way. But *you* decide: read the sentence without the bracketed material and see if it works." In the first half of the term, the students' papers were festooned with my brackets. Whole paragraphs got bracketed. But gradually the students learned to put mental brackets around their many different kinds of clutter, and by the end of the term I was returning papers to them that had hardly any brackets, or none. It was always a satisfying moment. Today many of those students are professional writers. "I still see your brackets," they tell me. "They're following me through life."

You can develop the same eye. Writing is clear and strong to the extent that it has no superfluous parts. (So is art and music and dance and typography and design.) You will really enjoy writing on a word processor when you see your sentences growing in strength, literally before your eyes, as you get rid of the fat. Be thankful for everything that you can throw away.

I was struck by how many phrases and sentences I wrote in this book that I later found I didn't need. Many of them hammered home a point that didn't need hammering because it had already been made. This kind of overwriting happens in almost everybody's first draft, and it's perfectly natural—the act of putting down our thoughts makes us garrulous. Luckily, the act of editing follows the act of writing, and this is where the word processor will bail you out. It intercedes at the point where the game can be won or lost. With its help I cut hundreds of unnecessary words and didn't replace them.

Hundreds of others were discarded because I later thought of a better word—one that caught more precisely or more vividly what I was trying to express. Here, again, a word processor encourages you to play. The English language is rich in words that convey an exact shade of meaning. Don't get stuck with a word that's merely good if you can find one that takes the reader by surprise with its color or aptness or quirkiness. Root around in your dictionary of synonyms and find words that are fresh. Throw them up on the screen and see how they look.

Also learn to play with whole sentences. If a sentence strikes you as awkward or ponderous, move your cursor to the space after the period and write a new sentence that you think is better. Maybe you can make it shorter. Or clearer. Maybe you can make it livelier by turning it into a question or otherwise altering its rhythm. Change the passive verbs into active verbs. (Passive verbs are the death of clarity and vigor.) Try writing two or three new versions of the awkward sentence and then compare them, or write a fourth version that combines the best elements of all three. Sentences come in an infinite variety of shapes and sizes. Find one that pleases you. If it's clear, and if it pleases you and expresses who you are, trust it to please other people. Then delete all the versions that aren't as good. Your shiny new sentence will jump into position and the rest of the paragraph will rearrange itself as quickly and neatly as if you had never pulled it apart.

Another goal that the word processor will help you to achieve is unity. No matter how carefully you write each sentence as you assemble a piece of writing, the final product is bound to have some ragged edges. Is the tone consistent throughout? And the point of view? And the pronoun? And the tense? How about the transitions? Do they pull the reader along, or is the piece jerky and disjointed? A good piece of writing should be harmonious from beginning to end in the voice of the writer and the flow of its logic. But the harmony usually requires some last-minute patching.

I've been writing this book by the bricklayer method, slowly and carefully. That's all very well as far as it goes—at the end of every chapter the individual bricks may look fine. But what about the wall? The only way to check your piece for unity is to go over it one more time from start to finish, preferably reading it aloud. See if you have executed all the decisions that you made before you started writing.

One such decision is in the area of tone. I decided, for instance, that I didn't want this book to be a technical manual. I'm not a technician; I'm a writer and an editor. The book wouldn't work if I expected the reader to identify with the process of mastering a new technology. He would have to identify with me. The book would be first of all a personal journey and only parenthetically a manual. I knew that this was a hybrid form and that its unities would never be wholly intact. Still, in going over each finished chapter I found places where the balance could be improved—where instructional detail smothered the writer and his narrative, or, conversely, where the writer intruded on the procedures he was trying to explain. With a word processor it was easy to make small repairs—perhaps just a change of pronoun and verb—that made the balance less uneven.

The instructional portions of the book posed a problem of their own—one that I had never faced before. My hope was to try to explain a technical process without the help of any diagrams or drawings. Would this be possible? It would be possible only if I kept remembering one fundamental fact: writing is linear and sequential. This may seem so obvious as to be insulting: everybody knows that writing is linear and sequential. Actually everybody doesn't know. Most people under thirty don't know. They have been reared since early childhood on television—a kaleidoscope of visual images flashed onto their brain—and it doesn't occur to them that sentence B must follow sentence A, and that sentence C must follow sentence B, or all the elegant sentences in the world won't add up to anything but confusion.

I mention this because word processors are going to be widely used by people who need to impart technical information: matters of operating procedure in business and banking, science and technology, medicine and health, education and government and dozens of other specialized fields. The information will only be helpful if readers can grasp it quickly and easily. If it's muddy they will get discouraged or angry, or both, and will stop reading.

You can avoid this dreaded fate for your message, whatever it is, by making sure that every sentence is a logical sequel to the one that preceded it. One way to approach this goal is to keep your sentences short. A major reason why technical prose becomes so tangled is that the writer tries to make one sentence do too many jobs. It's a natural hazard of the first draft. But the solution is simple: see that every sentence contains only one thought. The reader can accommodate only one idea at a time. Help him by giving him only one idea at a time. Let him understand A before you proceed to B.

In writing this book I was eager to explain the procedures that I had learned, and I would frequently lump several points together in one sentence. Later, editing what I had written, I asked myself if the procedure would be clear to someone who was puzzling through it for the first time— someone who hadn't struggled to figure the procedure out. Often I felt that it wouldn't be clear. I was giving the reader too much. He was being asked to picture himself taking various steps that were single and sequential, and that's how he deserved to get them.

I therefore divided all troublesome long sentences into two short sentences, or even three. It always gave me great pleasure. Not only is it the fastest way for a writer to get out of a quagmire that there seems to be no getting out of; I also like short sentences for their own sake. There's almost no more beautiful sight than a simple declarative sentence. This book is full of simple declarative sentences that have no punctuation and that carry one simple thought. Without a word pro-

cessor I wouldn't have chopped as many of them down to
their proper size, or done it with so little effort. This is one of
the main clarifying jobs that your machine can help you to
perform, especially if your writing requires you to guide the
reader into territory that is new and bewildering.

Not all my experiences, of course, were rosy. The machine
had disadvantages as well as blessings. Often, for instance, I
missed not being able to see more than twenty lines at a
time—to review what I had written earlier. If I wanted to
see more lines I had to "scroll" them back into view.

But even this wasn't as painful as I had thought it would
be. I found that I could hold in my head the gist of what I
had written and didn't need to keep looking at it. Was this
need, in fact, still another writer's hang-up that I could shed?
To some extent it was. I discovered, as I had at so many
other points in this journey, that various crutches I had always assumed I needed were really not necessary. I made a
decision to just throw them away and found that I could still
function. The only real hardship occurred when a paragraph
broke at the bottom of the screen. This meant that the first
lines of the paragraph were on one page and the rest were on
the next page, and I had to keep flicking the two pages back
and forth to read what I was writing. But again, it wasn't
fatal. I learned to live with it and soon took it for granted as
an occupational hazard.

The story that I've told in this chapter is personal and idio-
syncratic: how the word processor helped one writer to write
one book. In many of its details it's everybody's story. But all
writers have different methods and psychological needs.
Yours may be unlike mine in many ways. In which case,
you'll want to know: "What will the word processor do for
*me?*"

I have a few thoughts on the matter.

# 17.  The Act of Writing: Other Methods

The question about writing on a word processor that I've been asked most often goes something like this:

"What if I write a second draft and then think that maybe my first draft was better? Can I get it back and look at it? How about those different leads I tried that I didn't think were any good? Now I remember that one of them had a phrase I really liked. Maybe I can use it after all. Can I still do that? Or is it lost somewhere?"

The question (whatever form it takes) sums up all the fears that writers bring to the word processor. They assume that the machine couldn't possibly cater to their particular writing habits, which depend on their being able to retrieve and reshape a lot of material that they previously assembled. If anything, the machine will whisk what they write into its innards and they will never see it again.

I understand the paranoia. When everything is written down on paper it can be found and reviewed and put to use on some other piece of paper. But when words are mere shadows of light in an electronic box they offer no such security. Any writer worth his weight in anxiety can't help thinking: "Are my words *really* inside that box? Can I *really* get them back out and fiddle with them?"

In my own case this wasn't a concern. For one thing, I didn't save earlier drafts of my chapters. I just wrote and rewrote this book as I went along, not keeping any record of what I had replaced because I didn't like it and didn't want to see it again. I also wasn't working from a body of research that I had already gathered. The book just grew organically.

But most writers work from a more spacious design. Their method is to get a lot of material down on paper and then decide how to use it. They write out their notes and their research. They transcribe their interviews. They rough out some thoughts and impressions. They write some paragraphs that they know will belong in the middle of what they eventually write; they aren't hung up on starting at the beginning. And when they do write a first draft it's a hasty spilling out of sentences that they know aren't much good; they just want to get something said before they forget it.

All this is the normal and healthy activity of a writer getting warmed up, getting his adrenalin going, getting his ideas circling around in his head. Just the physical act of typing is a powerful source of energy—it summons from the subconscious mind a multitude of facts and memories that the writer needs at exactly that moment.

For such writers the word processor is as good a tool as it is for the tortoises like me who plod along a straight and narrow path. It invites you—if you're such a writer—to write freely, even with abandon, and to store a vast amount of material. There's no shortage of storage space: one eight-inch disk will hold 25,000 words. The only problem that you have to solve is one of access: how are you going to organize and index your material so that you can retrieve it quickly?

Here are several premises to start from.

First, accept the fact that your disks are now your files. If you want a printed copy of certain pages that are stored on a disk, you can print them from the disk. But try to get comfortable with the idea of having all your material available in one place: on your screen.

Also remember that you can put many different "documents" on one diskette—for example, twenty-five documents of one thousand words each, or fifty documents of five hundred words. Every document that you create has a different name. This gives you an indexing system. If you forget what documents are on your diskette you can ask the machine at any time to display an index of its contents. You can also keep a separate index—on a sheet of paper—that describes the documents more fully.

Remember, too, that every diskette, not just every document, has a different name. This gives you two systems of storing material—by document and by diskette. You can change the name of a document or a diskette at any time by using the Work Diskette menu. No name is irrevocable.

Also don't forget that you can make a duplicate of any diskette. Therefore you can always preserve your original.

Finally, remember that the keyboard has a key called MOVE, which will shift any chunk of writing from one place to another. You can move material within a paragraph, or from one page to another, or from one document to another, or even from one diskette to another.

How you use these various options will depend, of course, on how you like to work. There's almost no limit to the variety of projects that a word processor can help a writer to write, ranging from a simple article to a scholarly book or a doctoral dissertation with hundreds of footnotes. All you have to do is devise a system of storage and retrieval that will meet the needs of your particular project.

Assume that you're writing a fairly simple article by the

let-it-all-hang-out-on-the-first-draft method. You write rapidly, not fussing with grammar or punctuation, and reach the end with considerable relief—you have accomplished the crucial first step. You realize that your sloppy manuscript will need plenty of work. But it also has many sentences that you like. They have the spontaneity that comes from writing impulsively, and you don't want to lose them when you revise.

You can proceed in any of several ways. Most obviously, you can print a copy of your first draft and work from that when you rewrite. In this case, you might want to do your rewriting on your original "manuscript" on the screen—cutting, patching, punctuating, bringing order out of disarray. No matter how badly you mutilate it, you still have a printed copy of the original.

Or you might prefer to start your rewrite from scratch, not from the original. In which case, you would give the rewrite document a different name. Both the original and the first rewrite would therefore be on the same disk, and you could periodically call the original back to the screen for reference. You could also move whole paragraphs from the original to the rewrite—the paragraphs that contain those wonderful sentences that you like so much.

Another procedure would be to duplicate your original draft on a second diskette. That would preserve it intact. In fact, you might want to make that second diskette the repository for all your early drafts and notes. This would gratify the writer's compulsion not to throw away any material until the whole job is finished. It would be the electronic equivalent of the newspaperman's "spike"—the metal pin on which he impales everything that he no longer needs but that some primordial instinct tells him to save. Surprisingly often he's glad he saved it.

Going from the simple to the complex, assume that you're writing a long and scholarly book: a history, a biography, a textbook, a monograph, a scientific treatise. Such works are seldom just written from start to finish. They involve a prodigious accumulation of notes and data from which the book will later be distilled. The scholarly writer files all this material in manila folders under different subject headings.

With a word processor, the contents of the folder get filed instead on a disk. Half a dozen subjects might get filed on one diskette. Or, if the subject is big enough, it could occupy an entire diskette.

Assume that you're just getting started on your monumental history of the Civil War. You'll almost surely want to designate a separate diskette for "Lincoln," and one for "Slavery," and one for "Grant & the Union Generals," etc. On the "Lincoln" diskette you'll not only assemble your Lincoln research; you'll also write your Lincoln footnotes there and maybe even write some of your Lincoln chapters. You'll do the same thing on your "Grant" diskette, and on your "Lee & the South" diskette, and on your other diskettes, so that your book will gradually begin to exist in little pockets on various diskettes.

Then you'll put the book together, using the MOVE key to arrange the sections and the footnotes in their proper sequence. Then you'll give it continuity by writing the necessary transitions. Then, when ordinarily you would have to get the whole manuscript neatly retyped, you'll use the PRINT menu. Your printer will type a perfect manuscript of your book, perfectly paginated from beginning to end, with all the footnotes in place, and all you have to do is sit back and wait for your Pulitzer Prize.

When the time comes for a revised second edition, your job will be relatively easy. Just find the diskettes that contain your manuscript (you have wisely saved them) and summon onto the screen the pages where you want to insert the new material that your research has since turned up. Stitch the new in with the old—all those fresh insights about Lincoln's hat and Grant's beard—and when your printer types out another perfect manuscript nobody will even notice the seams.

For a scholar doing such a project the word processor is a miraculous helper. If your task as a writer is to assemble any big and unwieldy body of material, whatever the subject, you can save hundreds of hours of drudgery. Just turn yourself over to the machine's amazing ability to store, retrieve, revise and rearrange in proper order the countless fragments of your scholarship.

What other kinds of writers will the word processor help? Many other kinds kept occurring to me.

I often thought, for instance, of children. The new technology could erase the biggest obstacle that frustrates children learning how to write: the sheer labor of writing. Children are natural writers. Their heads are full of imagery and wonder and wordplay and free association; their use of language is fresh and unexpected. But their hands are far slower than their thoughts. The act of forming words with a pencil is hard, and the words that they painfully manage to form don't satisfy anybody—not the teacher, who wants them to be more legible and neat, and certainly not the child, who wishes that his words didn't look so childish. A writer at any age deserves a certain integrity for his writing.

A word processor would not only eliminate this problem; it would turn writing into a pleasure and would release creative energies that are now largely blocked. Children, of course, would have to learn to type at an earlier age. But typing is a skill that they'll always need; they might as well get an early start on it. I can't think of a quicker way to give them a sense of the enjoyment that comes from playing with

words—words in all their fanciful shapes and sizes and com-
binations—than to let them write on a screen where all
things are possible and all mistakes are instantly forgiven,
where the touch is light and the page forever tidy.

I can hear (as I write) the howls of the purists: give children a machine to write on and they will become machine-
like, separated from the personal environment that gives creative people their humanity. I don't believe it. There's no
law that says writing has to be onerous, any more than
housecleaning has to be done by broom in the age of the
vacuum cleaner. Besides, the word processor won't replace
the act of writing; it will only process the words that the
child still has to generate.

Not all educators would agree on such an early start. Some
of them feel that children would be most helped by word
processors in the sixth grade—at about age twelve—when
they are first being taught to revise what they have written.
The fact is that nobody knows; the technology is too new. I
only know that far too many children lose as they get older
the exuberance that made their younger writing so distinctive and appealing. Any machine that will postpone this process of drying up—and will let them continue to write with
freedom and risk—is a machine that parents and teachers
should take seriously.

I also think of poets. Maybe I shouldn't—poets and machines are supposed to be natural enemies. Still, no other
writer works in so constrained a form, or juggles words so
doggedly to make them fit that form, or slaves in such obedi-
ence to rhyme and meter, or gives such thought to arranging
the shape of a line to suggest to the eye what he hears in his
ear. Surely such a born fiddler with words will revel in a
machine that so liberates the act of fiddling.

I think of playwrights and screenwriters and novelists—all

the writers who deal in dialogue. Like most other kinds of writing, dialogue tends on the first draft to be a little long. Only by reading his lines aloud can the writer hear where he has missed the cadences and idioms of speech and made his talk too formal. On a word processor such near-misses can be instantly caught and fixed.

But you don't have to write a play, or a book, or a poem. You don't even have to write about Lincoln's hat and Grant's beard. The main thing—whether you're writing one page or five hundred—is to try to write clearly and warmly and well.

Writing is a personal transaction conducted on paper. It is one person talking to another person. Readers identify first with the person who is writing, not with what the person is writing about. Often, in fact, we will read about a subject that really doesn't interest us because we like the writer. We like the warmth or humor or humanity that he brings to his subject. We may think we are responding to the writer's "style"; actually we are responding to his personality as he expresses it in words.

The word processor will help you to achieve three cardinal goals of good writing—clarity, simplicity and humanity—if you make it your servant and not your master. Remember that it's only a machine, so don't be afraid of it. You'll even learn to like it. Take it from an American boy who always hated machines.

# 18.  The Final Step

It's now October and I'm at the end of my trip. It began when I called on Robert and Donna at IBM and told them I wanted to try to write a book on a word processor. They assured me that their system was user-friendly, and for this user it has been at least fairly friendly. My book is written and I have two disks to prove it. The first disk has 105 pages of writing and this one has twenty-seven pages. I also have a complete manuscript that I've printed on my printer.

But there's one last step to travel. I knew from the beginning that I wanted to use the new technology not only to write and edit my book, but to get it composed in type. I therefore decided that I would give my publisher my disks instead of a manuscript. This would save the time and money of having a phototypesetter retype what I had already typed. I didn't have to be a clairvoyant to see that writers will increasingly be bringing a disk—not paper—to the people who publish what they write. I would be Harper & Row's first electronic author.

When I finished the book I sent the manuscript—every chapter except this one, which I'm writing now—to the publisher for copy editing and proofreading. There the editors checked it for errors of typing. They also changed various words to make them conform to standard usage in such areas as numbers, names, hyphens and capitals. Their style, for instance, is to spell out numbers like "fifty-three" that I type as "53." They eliminate the hyphen that I put in words like "reexamine" and "absentmindedly." They italicize certain proper names that I type with quotation marks. They use lower case on certain words that I capitalize.

When they had marked all their changes they sent the manuscript back to me. The entire process took four or five days. I summoned the pages back onto my screen and made the changes at my keyboard. That took several hours. What's now on my two disks, therefore, is my final edited manuscript. If the book turns out to have any typographical errors, those errors were made by me.

I've also made a duplicate of the two corrected disks. I want a duplicate in case anything happens to the disks that I give to Harper & Row. But the duplicate will also be useful if I revise this edition to add new material or to correct anything that may be wrong. I'll only need to type what is being added and to delete what is being removed. The machine will put the revised manuscript in order and repaginate it.

I'd like to think that Harper & Row is eagerly awaiting my two disks. But in their heart of hearts they wish I were bringing them a manuscript. They are dismayed by this strange artifact that is about to arrive. They're in the business of publishing *writing*, after all, and have been since 1817. Writers are not supposed to come bearing software.

But I've told them that there's no turning back. We're in this together—love me, love my disks. We are going to turn those disks into type.

How will this be done? The disks will be given to a photo-typesetting company. There they will be programmed with specifications, provided by the designer, that will determine how the finished book will look. For instance: the book will be set in 11 point Caledonia type on a 14 point body, 23 picas wide. The pages will have 33 lines of type, except for pages that begin a chapter, which will have only 21 lines. There will be "running heads" and page numbers at the top of every page, except pages that begin a chapter. All paragraphs will be indented one em, no matter how erratically I have typed them, and all words that I have typed in capital letters will be set in small caps.

The specifications, in short, will be quite simple: routine matters of type, spacing and margins. But if this were a complex book—one that involved footnotes or statistical tables—the procedure would be the same. The designer would decide how he wanted all the footnotes and tables treated, and the typesetter would program the disks accordingly. The instructions would only have to be issued once; the system would execute them throughout.

After my disks have been given their typographical coding they will be fed into a computer that has in its memory bank a huge assortment of typefaces in all sizes. From that bank the impulses on my disk will summon photo images of the individual letters of 11 point Caledonia type, picking the letters and spaces—at fantastic speed—to form words. The computer will arrange the words in lines 23 picas wide, hyphenating where necessary. It will put 33 lines on every page, except on pages that begin and end a chapter, and it will also summon the type for the chapter titles, the "running heads" and the page numbers.

When the computer has worked its way through the thirty-five thousand words that my two disks contain, the images that it has generated will be fed to a camera, which will produce film negatives of all the pages—the preface and eighteen consecutive chapters. These negatives will then be given to a printer, along with the negatives of the title page and the other introductory pages. From these negatives the printer will make offset plates, from which the book will be printed. (Offset is a lithographic printing process.) The whole procedure—converting my disks to negatives ready for the printer—will take about a week. Ordinarily, publishers allow at least three months for an author's manuscript to be typeset and organized into pages for the printer.

This doesn't mean that I can't have one final look. The typesetter will provide a set of page proofs for the publisher and me to check—positive prints made from the film negative. If we see any errors, they can still be corrected.

Although the book will go directly "into pages," bypassing the usual first step of getting unpaged galley proofs, that first step is still possible. You can ask for galleys, for instance, if your book has many disparate elements that you want to measure and assemble in their proper position: type, pictures, captions, maps, graphs, tables, extracts, footnotes.

But even that stage is just about obsolete. The technology of "computer graphics" is moving so fast that art directors can now lay out entire books or magazines by sitting at a keyboard and playing video games. What this will mean for a writer or an editor with a word processor is a future that will save time and labor in countless ways that I've only begun to glimpse. Right now it's enough that I could write and set a book and get it published in less than a year.

Tomorrow, when I deliver my book to Harper & Row, dodging the ghosts of Herman Melville and Thomas Wolfe and dozens of other writers who walked through the streets of Manhattan looking like writers, nobody will mistake me for a member of the clan. I'll have no fat manuscript—just two small disks. I'll take the elevator up to my editor's office and hand him the disks. He will expect me to say something ceremonial—a few words befitting the completion of a voyage across unknown seas.

"Don't bend them," I'll say.